The Assault on Indian Tribalism

Wilcomb E. Washburn

Smithsonian Institution

The America's Alternatives Series
Edited by **Harold M. Hyman**

The Assault on Indian Tribalism:
The General Allotment Law (Dawes Act) of 1887

J. B. Lippincott Company
Philadelphia/New York/Toronto

Copyright © 1975 by J. B. Lippincott Company. All rights reserved.
This book is fully protected by copyright, and, with the exception of brief extracts for review, no part of it may be reproduced in any form, by print, photoprint, microfilm, or any other means, without written permission of the publisher.

ISBN 0-397-47337-0
Library of Congress Catalog Card Number 74-23141
Printed in the United States of America
1 3 5 7 9 8 6 4 2

Library of Congress Cataloging in Publication Data

Washburn, Wilcomb E.
  Assault on Indian tribalism.

  (The America's alternatives series)
  Bibliography: p.
  1. Indians of North America—Land tenure. I. Title.
KF5660.W38   343'.73'025   74-23141
ISBN 0-397-47337-0

Contents

Foreword vii

PART ONE　The Assault on Indian Tribalism　1

1　The Impulse for Reform: Alternatives in Plan and Policy　3
Indian Policy: The Alternatives 3　*The Indian Rights Sympathizers Organize* 5　*The Indians' Position on Severalty* 8　*The Role of the "Experts"* 10　*The Role of the Humanitarians* 12

2　The Decision for Compulsory Allotment of Land　15
"The Reservation Must Go" 16　*Indian "Benefits" and White Interests* 18　*The "Inevitable" Breakup of the Reservations* 21　*Allotment and Citizenship: "Adopting the Habits of Civilized Life"* 22　*Towards a Coercive Stance* 24

EPILOGUE　Impact of the Decision　28
Indian Losses, White Gains 28　*Belated and Halfhearted Regret* 29

PART TWO　Documents of the Decision　33

1　"The Main Purpose of This Bill is Not to Help the Indian"　35

2　Senate Debate on Severalty　41

3 Senator Dawes Seeks a Solution 46
4 The Support of the Indian Rights Association for Land in Severalty Bill 49
5 The Beginnings of Compulsory Allotment 53
6 Pressures for "Prompt" and Compulsory Allotment 56
7 A Protest Against Forced Allotment 58
8 "Shall We Persist in a Policy that has Failed?" 61
9 The General Allotment Act of 1887 ("The Dawes Act") 68

PART THREE   Bibliographic Essay   75

Foreword

"When you judge decisions, you have to judge them in the light of what there was available to do it," noted Secretary of State George C. Marshall to the Senate Committees on the Armed Services and Foreign Relations in May 1951.[1] In this spirit, each volume in the "America's Alternatives" series examines the past for insights which History—perhaps only History—is peculiarly fitted to offer. In each volume the author seeks to learn why decision makers in crucial public policy or, more rarely, private choice situations adopted a course and rejected others. Within this context of choices, the author may ask what influence then-existing expert opinion, administrative structures, and budgetary factors exerted in shaping decisions? What weights did constitutions or traditions have? What did men hope for or fear? On what information did they base their decisions? Once a decision was made, how was the decision maker able to enforce it? What attitudes prevailed toward nationality, race, region, religion, or sex, and how did these attitudes modify results?

We freely ask such questions of the events of our time. This "America's Alternatives" volume transfers appropriate versions of such queries to the past.

In examining those elements that were a part of a crucial historical decision, the author has refrained from making judgments based upon attitudes, information, or values that were not current at the time the decision was made. Instead, as much as possible he or she has explored the past in terms of data and prejudices known to persons contemporary to the event.

---

[1] U.S., Congress, Senate, Hearings Before the Committees on the Armed Services and the Foreign Relations of the United States, *The Military Situation in the Far East*, 82 Cong., 2d sess., Part I, p. 382. Professor Ernest R. May's "Alternatives" volume directed me to this source and quotation.

Nevertheless, the following reconstruction of one of America's major alternative choices speaks implicitly and frequently, explicitly to present concerns.

In form, this volume consists of a narrative and analytical historical essay (Part One), within which the author has identified (i.e., *Alternative 1*, etc.) the choices which he believes were actually before the decision makers with whom he is concerned.

Part Two of this volume contains, in whole or part, the most appropriate source documents that illustrate the Part One Alternatives. The Part Two Documents and Part One essay are keyed for convenient learning use (i.e., references in Part One will direct readers to appropriate Part Two Documents). The volume's Part Three offers users further guidance in the form of a Bibliographic Essay.

A century ago, as Americans enjoyed the centennial of national independence, they paid relatively little attention—far too little, as events have disclosed—to efforts then under way to rationalize Indian-white relationships. Americans preparing to celebrate their nation's bicentennial in 1976 owe a duty of reflection on aspects of their past that, as difficult and urgent problems, persist into the present. In 1973 and 1974, violence between militant Indians and federal officers dramatized the fact that agreeable solutions are not yet in hand.

Dr. Wilcomb Washburn is an eminent student of American Indian history. His analysis and documents in this volume offer unprecedented opportunity for a review of one of the most significant efforts by white Americans to reshape the lives of American Indians in ways conformable to white perceptions.

Harold M. Hyman
Rice University

Part One

The Assault on Indian Tribalism

1

The Impulse for Reform: Alternatives in Plan and Policy

Indian Policy: The Alternatives

The General Allotment Act (see Document 9), also known as the Dawes Severalty Act, became law in 1887. It was the culmination of a decade of intense concern on the part of an increasingly dominant white majority over the future status of the increasingly helpless Indian minority within the United States. The act did not simply rearrange the landholding system of the Indians. It dealt, sometimes only in a tentative or partial way, with all aspects of the relationship between white men and red: it determined how much land the red man would retain and how much the white man would acquire; it determined whether past treaties would be honored or violated; it determined how much authority the tribe would retain and how much the Indian individual would acquire; it determined what type of law the Indian would be subjected to; and it determined whether or not he would become an American citizen or remain an alien in his own country. The act did not determine all these questions fully and finally; but it did confront them directly, even if it answered them only partially.

The present volume will treat the various alternatives faced by legislators on the road to the compromise legislation that finally emerged. The alternatives facing Americans concerned with Indian policy in the 1880s may be stated as follows:

Alternative 1: destroy the status quo: violate, or render inoperative, treaty guarantees; destroy tribal integrity; kill or remove Indians, or wait for them to die off.

Alternative 2: maintain the status quo: support existing treaty guarantees, tribal integrity, and the right of tribes to hold land in common; protect the individual Indian against white aggression.

Alternative 3: change the status quo by voluntary agreement of tribes leading gradually to individual allotment of lands and adoption of "civilized" ways.

Alternative 4: change the status quo by involuntary means by destroying tribal autonomy, and forcing Indians rapidly into individual allotment of lands, subjection to the white man's law, and mandatory citizenship.

Alternative 5: any of the above alternatives, but with the addition of benefits to white farmers greedy for Indian land, to white miners eager to exploit Indian mineral wealth, and to railroad companies anxious for Indian land and rights-of-way.

Was Alternative 1 possible in a civilized, Christian nation in the nineteenth century? The answer is yes. Christianity and "civilization" have not always been able to save the aboriginal inhabitants of lands settled by Europeans; indeed, they have sometimes provided justifications for their destruction. But neither Christianity nor "civilization" needs to be called upon to explain or to justify some of the cruelty practiced against the native peoples of North America. The reduction of the California Indian population in the second half of the nineteenth century was accomplished with a casual and lawless brutality which was unequalled by the record of any previous period of American history, and was exceeded only by the savage destruction of millions of natives in Central and South America by the onslaughts of the sixteenth-century Spanish conquerors.[1]

Indian lands, though guaranteed by sacred treaties, were, in the 1870s, increasingly violated by lawless whites whenever reports of wealth to be found inside the reservations were received. Colonel Richard I. Dodge, in his book *Our Wild Indians*, published in 1882, predicted that "it is a mere question of time when all the reservations will be overrun." The Black Hills of South Dakota, reserved to the Sioux by the Treaty of 1868, were unceremoniously entered by George A. Custer's Seventh Cavalry Regiment in 1874. Custer's reconnaissance in force was soon followed by an invasion of white miners, lured by tales of mineral wealth. The government sought to buy the area from the Sioux, but the tribe refused and prepared for war. The initial outcome of the confrontation shocked the nation, long used to the success of white arms. Custer and a large portion of his regiment were killed on June 25, 1876, by Sioux and Northern Cheyenne warriors under Crazy Horse, Sitting Bull, and other tribal leaders. Success was short lived, however. The Indians were gradually killed, imprisoned, driven out of the country, or exiled to the Indian Territory (the present State of Oklahoma): "peace" was restored to the Plains.[2]

Meanwhile, in the Oregon Territory, another tragedy was playing itself out. Young Joseph, who succeeded his father as Chief of the Wallowa Nez Perces in 1871, attempted to hold on to his traditional homeland in the Wallowa Valley, which the United States claimed had been ceded to it by his father in the treaty of 1863. As stockmen and settlers began taking up land in the valley, tensions mounted. Violence was avoided for several years while negotiations to resolve the controversy took place, but, finally, in 1876, an Indian was killed by settlers and war broke out. Joseph's band, after a brilliant military effort against the United States Army, was defeated in 1877.[3]

The lands of the Ute Indians of Colorado, like those of the Sioux in South Dakota, were encroached upon by whites in the 1870s, especially after the discovery of silver deposits near Leadville. Ouray, the great Ute chief, sought to avoid conflict, but discovered that earlier treaty guarantees were of little avail against the aggressive invaders. The pressure of the miners was compounded by the cultural pressure of the Ute agent, Nathaniel C. Meeker, who sought to coerce the Utes to "civilized" ways. In 1878, bitter over indignities he had suffered at the hands of the Indians, Meeker called for army support. The Utes insisted that the soldiers stay out of the reservation; on their refusal, they were badly mauled by the Indians and the agent killed. Reinforcements came hastily to the rescue of the soldiers, and the Utes were humbled. Colorado citizens demanded that the Utes be forcibly removed from the state, and a Ute Commission was set up to negotiate their fate in the face of these threats.[4]

It will be apparent from the foregoing discussion that the preservation of the status quo (*Alternative 2*) was probably the least likely alternative facing Americans at the end of the 1870s, because that status quo depended upon law and morality which no longer had the support of Indian power or white conviction. Treaties negotiated with tribes when they held the power to devastate the frontier seemed less compelling to whites when the Indians had lost the power to exact bloody sanctions for white noncompliance. Promises to respect tribal integrity and autonomy seemed harder to keep when tribal organizations blocked dissolution of the large Indian landholdings desired by white settlers. There were a few isolated voices who insisted that treaties should be honored even though they could be broken with impunity. Among those voices was that of A. B. Meacham, one of the commissioners who had negotiated with the Modoc leader "Captain Jack" during the Modoc War, 1872-1873, and who had been wounded four times and left for dead with the other commissioners murdered during the negotiations. Meacham started a journal named *The Council Fire* in 1878 in which, as one grievously wronged by the Indians, he was able to argue with particular effectiveness that their rights be respected.[5]

The Indian Rights Sympathizers Organize

The series of bloody confrontations that occurred during the 1870s, which had at first stimulated fear, evoked increasing sympathy for the red man as his power (and with it white fear) declined. A particularly heartrending event converted much of this latent sympathy into organizational muscle. That event was the removal of the Ponca Indians. The land guaranteed to the Ponca Indians by the treaty of 1865 had been included, owing to a bureaucratic mistake, within the reservation authorized to the Sioux by the treaty of 1868. The government's response to Sioux attempts to force the Poncas from the lands in the 1870s was to pack up the latter and send them, in 1877, against their will, to the Indian Territory, where many died of disease and all suffered from the unfamiliar hot climate. In 1879, Standing

Bear led a band of Poncas back from the Indian Territory toward their original homeland in Nebraska. The army was called in to prevent the move.[6] Indian rights advocates, hitherto unorganized or only loosely organized, came together in organized groups determined to halt the shameful treatment of the Poncas in particular, and of the American Indians in general.

The Boston Indian Citizenship Association, which included Republican Governor John D. Long, poet and novelist Helen Hunt Jackson, and Massachusetts' Republican Senator Henry L. Dawes, grew out of the Ponca affair. The Women's National Indian Association of Philadelphia was also organized late in 1879 to help the Indian, and by 1886 numbered sixty branch organizations in twenty-seven states. The powerful Indian Rights Association, also based in Philadelphia, was organized shortly thereafter, in 1882.[7]

The newly organized Indian humanitarian organizations were confronted not only with the evidence of injustice evident in the Ponca, Ute, and Nez Perce affairs, but, in April 1879, the commissioner of Indian Affairs notified President Hayes of the existence of a plan hatched by citizens in surrounding states to seize Indian lands in the Indian Territory by force. President Hayes was encouraged to issue proclamations to forestall such an eventuality, but the pattern of white aggression and oppression of the Indians seemed increasingly evident to the humanitarian reformers.[8]

The reformers soon concluded that advocacy of the status quo (*Alternative 2*), however desirable, was not enough to protect the Indian from the incessant attacks upon him. However appealing the pleas of Standing Bear, Chief Joseph, or Ouray might be to white men and women of good will in the East (where most of the reform organizations were centered), they could not hope to turn back the hatred and greed of thousands of demanding westerners. Therefore, the reformers sought to present a scheme by which the Indian would be offered a new role which he could more easily defend against the onslaughts of his enemies (*Alternative 3: Voluntary change*). Principal among the schemes devised for the purpose was allotment of land in severalty, that is, the assignment to each individual Indian of a fee simple (white man's) title to a fixed number of acres of the land traditionally held as the possession of the entire tribe.

The doctrine of severalty was not new. It had been urged upon the Indians almost from the time of the formation of the republic, and had been incorporated in numerous treaties with Indian tribes in the first half of the nineteenth century. The Board of Indian Commissioners, a civilian board of distinguished citizens formed in 1869 to advise the government on Indian policy, repeatedly urged severalty upon the policy makers. As the board stated in its annual report for 1877, it had recommended "the division of lands now held in common, and the endowment of each Indian family with a permanent home" every year since the board was organized, "and scarcely a report of the Secretary of the Interior, or of the Commissioner of Indian Affairs, can be opened without finding the same recommendation." Although Congress failed to act upon the general allotment bills introduced for the first time in 1879, it was ready to authorize division of lands in severalty as part of the agreement to settle the Ute controversy. Many congressmen voted for the Ute bill, but did so as an alternative to war rather than because of a commitment to severalty for other reasons.[9]

Ezra A. Hayt, appointed commissioner of Indian Affairs in 1879 after serving as a member of the Board of Indian Commissioners, sent Carl Schurz, secretary of the interior, a draft severalty bill in 1879 with a letter recommending its submission to Congress. Hayt emphasized in his letter that "the experience of the Indian Department for the past fifty years goes to show that the government is impotent to protect the Indians on their reservations, especially when held in common, from the encroachments of its own people, whenever a discovery has been made rendering the possession of their lands desirable by the whites." Hayt expressed his conviction that by the adoption of such a measure "the race can be led in a few years to a condition where they may be clothed with citizenship and left to their own resources to maintain themselves as citizens of the republic."[10]

Following consultation between the chairman of the Indian Affairs Committee of the Senate and the commissioner of Indian Affairs, the outline of an allotment bill was determined.[11] The Indian Affairs Committee of the House of Representatives, to whom similar bills had been submitted for study, found itself in disagreement on the expediency and morality of the legislation. In its report of May 28, 1880, a majority of the committee supported the purposes of the bill, but a minority report challenged the conclusions of the majority (see Document 1).

Secretary of the Interior Carl Schurz continued to promote the idea of a severalty bill in his report of November 1, 1880, in which he expressed his "firm belief" that to own land in severalty, with a firm title to their farms inalienable for a certain number of years, was necessary for the progress of the Indians. Schurz reported that Indians were increasingly asking for a white man's title to their lands.[12]

Helen Hunt Jackson, writing to Henry Wadsworth Longfellow, noted that Schurz's reference to the "'encouraging symptom'" that Indians were "'asking for their lands in severalty'" was "a fair specimen of his hypocrisies." Mrs. Jackson was outraged at the praise heaped on Schurz as a friend of the Indian. Although once his admirer, she had come to the conclusion that Schurz was a liar.

> I wish also to tell you [she wrote to Oliver Wendell Holmes on March 2, 1881] that the famous Severalty Bill which he framed, and introduced, was, as he framed it, an infamous Bill. It, as White Eagle said 'plucked the Indian like a bird.' And the minute that Bill was, thanks to the Mass. Senators & to Senator Morgan, [of Alabama] so *amended*, that it could have been passed without danger to the Indian, and without the profit to *land speculators* originally afforded in it—that minute, the men in charge of the Bill, & Schurz being back of them—*ceased to push it*—refused to bring it up! This I know, for I was in Washington and watched it all.[13]

Two significant books lent weight to the renewed concern with the plight of the American Indian. George W. Manypenny, commissioner of Indian

Affairs in the 1950s, brought out in 1880 *Our Indian Wards*, which recounted the sorry history of Indian-white relations. In the following year Helen Hunt Jackson published *A Century of Dishonor*, an even more forceful denunciation of United States Indian policy. "So long as there remains on our frontier one square mile of land occupied by a weak and helpless owner," Mrs. Jackson wrote, "there will be a strong and unscrupulous frontiersman ready to seize it, and a weak and unscrupulous politician who can be hired for a vote or for money, to back him."[14]

The Indians' Position on Severalty

Although the evidence of history, and even of official reports of the results of earlier attempts at allotment, suggest that the overwhelming majority of Indians opposed the breakup of the tribal system, the Indian voice was either not heard, not heeded, or falsely reported. It is possible that many legislators were genuinely deceived by the assertion that (as the commissioner of Indian Affairs wrote in his annual report for the year 1880), "The demand for title to lands in severalty by the reservation Indians is almost universal." Senator Nathaniel Hill of Colorado, in quoting the commissioner, wondered whether "it is possible that the Commissioner of Indian Affairs is trying to deceive Congress and to put off upon the country a lie; but it certainly is strangely in conflict with the statements made by my colleague and others, that the Indians are almost unanimously opposed to it, and that they never can be brought to submit to it."[15]

The claim that Indians were clamoring for land in severalty had been asserted in the 1870s in debates over bills for allotment of land in severalty in particular areas. When a commission appointed by Congress in 1878 recommended the establishment of a territorial government in the Indian Territory, the commission maintained that there was Indian support for severalty. A. B. Meacham, editor of *The Council Fire*, vigorously opposed the plan. Having travelled extensively in the Indian Territory, Meacham asserted that, "We found not to exceed twenty persons who expressed a desire for territorial government and division of lands, and of these not one was either Cherokee, Chickasaw, Choctaw, Creek or Seminole Indian by blood." Meacham had no objection to honoring a genuine Indian request for a breakup of the tribal holdings if that should be the wish of the Indians themselves. But, he asserted, "It is cowardly for us to force these people under a government they do not want." It was particularly disgraceful, Meacham noted, for the good of the Indian to be asserted as the purpose of the division, and for sacred treaties to be violated to achieve it.[16]

Because of the continued, vocal opposition of the five civilized tribes of the Indian Territory to allotment, they were excluded from the general allotment act as it was eventually passed (see Document 9, section 8); the omission of the most advanced Indians from the provisions of a bill allegedly in the interests of those Indians most advanced in "civilization" did not escape the notice of some. Allotment was eventually forced on the Indians in the Indian Territory by the Curtis Act of 1898 and the Burke Act of 1906.[17] Early severalty bills normally proposed gradual allotment, usually with the consent of the Indians, and usually with the guarantee of a tribal patent (*Alternative 3: Voluntary Change*). The severalty bills introduced in the Congress in 1879 did not come to a vote before the end of the session. Reintroduced in 1880 in the Forty-sixth Congress, the severalty bills were discussed most thoroughly during the final days of January, 1881. The debate on the Coke bill (Senator Richard Coke of Texas had taken charge of the Senate severalty bill) was the most comprehensive airing that the allotment proposal was to receive in Congress. Portions of the debate are reproduced in Document 2. The legislation was favored by its proponents as essential to the Indian's permanent advancement in civilization.

The advocates of a general severalty law acted in ignorance or defiance of previous experience with severalty as applied to the Indians. As Henry M. Teller, senator from Colorado, put it in his speech of January 20, 1881 (see Document 2), "in the last thirty-six years we have made sixty-odd treaties with Indians, and all of them provided that they might take land in severalty, and in a majority of them that the Indians should take lands in severalty." Common sense, and historical evidence, indicated that the Indian did not generally wish to take land in severalty and, if he did take it, he frequently lost it to designing whites. Severalty legislation, though supported by public sentiment and presumably "all the intelligence and all the virtue of the country," was, Teller declared, fundamentally wrong.[18]

"If I stand alone in the Senate," Teller went on, "I want to put upon the record my prophecy in this matter, that when thirty or forty years shall have passed and these Indians shall have parted with their title, they will curse the hand that was raised professedly in their defense to secure this kind of legislation, and if the people who are clamoring for it understood Indian character, and Indian laws, and Indian morals, and Indian religion, they would not be here clamoring for this at all." Teller, a westerner, was not an advocate of the status quo for Indians. He believed that Indians must be "managed" in some fashion by the dominant white society, but he felt that legislation based on ignorance of their cultural heritage would not have the intended effect.[19]

Equally perceptive about the wrongheadedness of severalty legislation, and more anxious to safeguard the existing life of the Indian tribes, was the pioneer American ethnologist, Lewis H. Morgan. Morgan, in his study of *Houses and House-Life of the American Aborigines*, published in 1881, at the time of the great debate in the Congress on the severalty question, urged that the policy of severalty, with the power of alienation to white men even after a period of twenty-five years, "never be adopted by any National Administration, as it is fraught with nothing but mischief to the Indian tribes." The inevitable result for the Indian, he predicted, "would unquestionably be, that in a very short time he would divest himself of every foot of land and fall into poverty." The record of the past, Morgan noted, demonstrated the probability of this result; better to train the Indians to he herdsmen than to attempt to force them to become individual farmers.[20]

The early draft legislation varied in the degree to which Indian consent was necessary before allotment was applied (*Alternative 4: Coerced Change*). Some of the early bills calling for severalty required the consent of two-thirds of the males of the tribe twenty-one years old and upwards before the legislation would apply to any tribe. This provision was persistently criticized both on the grounds that it made an act of Congress subject to the veto of one-third of an Indian tribe and thus was demeaning to the majesty of the Congress, and that it put an arbitrary power in the hands of two-thirds of a tribe to "break down and destroy the vested rights of the balance of the tribe." During the debate of January, 1881, Senator John Tyler Morgan of Alabama even produced a letter—allegedly written by an Indian girl—which denounced the two-thirds rule as preventing individual Indians who desired to settle on a farm and improve it from doing so without the consent of the remaining two-thirds.[21]

The Role of the "Experts"

Senator Morgan, a proponent of the bill, sought to reinforce his argument by the expert testimony of Major John Wesley Powell, head of the Smithsonian Institution's Bureau of Ethnology. Powell had perhaps greater knowledge of the Indians of the western United States than any other white American at the time. He sought to give Senator Morgan a quick account of Indian culture and values, even to the explanation that "the occupation of lands in severalty is opposed to the customary laws, traditions, and religion of primitive tribal society." Yet Powell went beyond description to assume the role of advocate. He accepted the validity of "civilization" as a goal for Indians, and with that goal the necessity of creating individual property rights. "No measure," he asserted of the severalty bill then under consideration, "could be devised more efficient for the ultimate civilization of the Indians of this country than one by which they could successfully and rapidly obtain lands in severalty;..." Indeed, Powell, after a personal conversation with the senator, followed up his earlier letter with another which warned that it would be "disastrous" if the law prevented any Indian from taking an allotment until a two-thirds vote of his tribe sanctioned it.[22] Whether Powell felt constrained as a member of a quasi-governmental institution to toady to a powerful senator can be doubted. Powell was a forceful and outspoken man. He undoubtedly believed that the Indian culture as he knew it must change before the advance of civilization.

A. B. Meacham, editor of *The Council Fire*, commenting upon the Coke bill, favored the intent of the legislation as "essential to permanent advancement in civilization." However, *The Council Fire* opposed any attempt to force severalty upon the Indians. "The theory of force is all wrong." If the Indians wished to hold their lands in common "as have any of the hundreds of corporations and communities of white men that cover large tracts of our common country," they should be allowed to. It was only from "necessity," and want of a better title, the *Council Fire* noted, that the Indian asked for severalty.[23]

Meacham insisted that reforms must come when the Indian was ready for them.

We would have school houses built whenever the Indian demanded them, and schools established as fast as they were acceptable, and not before or faster. We would not make education compulsory. . . . When he is ready for a white man's house, *teach* him how to build one for himself. . . . Build it for him and compel him to quit his tepee, and he will burn the house and go to the tepee as soon as your back is turned. Mark out his land, plant monuments to designate the boundaries and give him a deed for it, he will tear down the monuments and burn the deed before your very eyes; but when he is ready he will ask for a home to himself; he will watch the monuments that mark the boundaries, he will treasure your deed as a sacred security; he will protect his home with his life.[24]

Alice Fletcher, a proper Boston lady who devoted her life to the study of the Indian and became one of the pioneer women anthropologists in the country, was galvanized into action in support of severalty legislation shortly after going to live among the Omaha Indians of Nebraska. The Omahas, stimulated by the sad history of the removal of the Ponca Indians from their home on the Niobrara river to the Indian Territory in 1879 against their will, feared that they in turn might be dispossessed from their homes. When some of the Ponca tribe under Standing Bear attempted to return to their homeland in 1879 and were rounded up by U.S. soldiers and carried back to the dreaded "hot country," the fate of these near neighbors to the Omaha "brought terror to every Omaha family," as Miss Fletcher later reported. The Poncas, thinking their own homes in danger, consulted white lawyers concerning the validity of the certificates of allotment of land which many of them had taken out in accordance with the treaty of 1835. They were told that the certificates carried no patent rights and were, therefore, subject to repudiation. Miss Fletcher thereupon commenced a campaign to obtain "strong paper"—titles in fee—for the Omahas. Her first act was to assemble statements from many Omaha Indians, which she incorporated in a memorial to the Senate of the United States. The memorial noted how the signers had taken out certificates of allotment of land, how each farmed from five to fifty acres, and how some had built houses on the lands, for which they now requested a clear and full title. They labored, they stated, "with discouragement of heart, knowing that our farms are not our own, and that any day we may be forced to leave the lands on which we have worked."[25]

The ball set in motion by Alice Fletcher resulted in the act of August 7, 1882, by which 76,000 acres were allotted with secure titles to 1,179 Omahas, the United States holding the patent in trust for twenty-five years. That portion of the reservation which was not held for individual allotments was offered for sale to whites.[26]

Philip C. Garrett, commissioner of public charities of the state of Pennsylvania, felt he was complimenting Miss Fletcher by saying that "her philanthropy swallowed up her anthropoligy" in the sense that, in the movement to obtain general severalty legislation, she did not insist upon the preservation of traditional Indian folkways at the expense of progress. A more recent observer, anthropologist Nancy O. Lurie, has concluded that "it is possible that if Alice Fletcher had studied the Omaha thoroughly, as she later did, instead of plunging first into the matter of lands, she would have sought some other solution to the Indians' economic problems than the one she brought with her into her field work." Yet, Lurie concludes, "Fletcher, for all her misguided benevolence, must at least be respected for regarding the welfare of the people she studied as her primary obligation."[27]

Senator Henry Dawes of Massachusetts, whose name was to grace the severalty act finally passed in 1887, was at the time of the Omaha severalty act a foe of rapid and compulsory allotment of lands. In a letter of September 19, 1882, sent by him to the outspoken Henry M. Teller, who had left the Senate and had become secretary of the interior (see document 3), Dawes ridiculed the idea of setting up the Indians in individual allotments and expecting them to "stand alone" with any success. Yet Dawes's willingness to be shaped by the forces playing upon the Indian rather than by his own convictions on what should be done (he cheerfully admitted he had no plan of his own to offer) was clearly expressed. He sought to reconcile the "irresistible forces driving the Indians in upon us" with his philanthropic concern for their welfare, but eagerly looked for direction from others as to the proper definition of that concern.[28]

The Role of the Humanitarians

Thoreau's comment that, if he knew that someone was coming to do him good, he would run for his life, is applicable to the role of humanitarians in regard to the American Indian. When a veritable phalanx of philanthropists turned their minds to helping the Indian in the post-Civil War period, his fate was sealed. One of the expressions of this philanthropic concern was the annual Lake Mohonk Conference held at Lake Mohonk in Ulster County, New York, "in behalf of the Civilization and Legal Protection of the Indians of the United States." Organized in 1883 by the Quaker Albert K. Smiley as a way of bringing together those individuals most concerned about solving the Indian "problem," with the purpose of hammering out agreements on needed reforms, which could then be publicized and lobbied for, the meetings were a great success. Representatives from government, universities, churches, and reform organizations were able, in the relaxed atmosphere of Lake Mohonk, to resolve differences of opinion and plot general strategy. Thus, in the carefully prepared 1884 meeting, the members were informed, by the presentation of Miss Alice C. Fletcher, that the Indians were capable of becoming citizens with individual allotments of land which they could farm capably. The conference then went on to resolve that "the organization of the Indians in tribes is, and has been, one of the most serious hindrances to the advancement of the Indian toward civilization, and that every effort should be made to secure the disintegration of all tribal organizations;..."

Although making a bow to existing treaty commitments, the conference resolved, "That to all Indians who desire to hold their land in severalty allotments should be made without delay; and that to all other Indians like allotments should be made so soon as practicable."[29]

The conference was interested in supporting a proposed bill in Congress: the Coke bill (48th Congress, 1st sess. S. 48), which was entitled an "Act to provide for the allotment of lands in severalty to Indians on the various reservations and to extend the protection of the laws of the States and Territories over the Indians, and for other purposes." The conference was concerned with how to promote the bill and to secure its passage. An example of the way in which the sharp edges and differences were smoothed and a united front presented to the government and to the public at large occurred in the discussions over the bill. Miss Fletcher, upon whose testimony the reformers relied to demonstrate the capacity of the Indians to be successful individual farmers, "hesitated to speak against a bill so warmly approved, but had little faith in general legislation on such a subject." She pointed out the unseen difficulties. One hundred and sixty acres of land—the amount specified in the bill to be allotted—was adequate in some places, but inadequate in others. Some Indians would not wish to be farmers, but traders. Education would be vitally necessary to convince the Indians to do what the reformers wished. In sum, Miss Fletcher feared that a general bill would do as much harm as good. But unable to move her fellow delegates on such "details," Miss Fletcher went along with the conference in approving the Coke bill "as the best practical measure yet brought before Congress for the preservation of the Indian from aggression, for the disintegration of the tribal organizations and for the ultimate breaking up of the injurious reservation system."[30]

Notes

1. Robert F. Heizer and Alan J. Almquist, *The Other Californians: Prejudice and Discrimination under Spain, Mexico, and the United States to 1920* (Berkeley: University of California Press, 1971).
2. Col. Richard I. Dodge, *Our Wild Indians: Thirty-Three Years' Personal Experience Among the Red Men of the Great West* (Hartford, Conn., 1882; reprint ed., New York: Archer House, 1959), p. 648; Dee Brown, *Bury My Heart at Wounded Knee: An Indian History of the American West* (New York: Holt, Rinehart and Winston, 1970), pp. 273-313; Robert M. Utley, *The Custer Legend* (New Haven, Conn.: Yale University Press, 1962).
3. Alvin M. Josephy, Jr., *The Nez Perce Indians and the Opening of the Northwest* (New Haven, Conn.: Yale University Press, 1965).
4. A. B. Meacham, editorial observation on the Ute Commission of 1880, in *The Council Fire* 3, no. 9 (September 1, 1880): 130. See also Brown, *Bury My Heart at Wounded Knee*, pp. 367-89.
5. Brown, *Bury My Heart at Wounded Knee*, pp. 219-40.
6. Robert Winston Mardock, *The Reformers and the American Indian* Columbia: University of Missouri Press, 1971), pp. 168-72.
7. Ibid., pp. 197-200.
8. Ibid., p. 201.

14   THE IMPULSE FOR REFORM

9. *Ninth Annual Report of the U.S. Board of Indian Commissioners for the Year 1877* (Washington, 1878), p. 7; Mardock, *The Reformers*, pp. 212-15.
10. Quoted in Francis Paul Prucha, ed., *Americanizing the American Indians: Writings by the "Friends of the Indian" 1880-1900* (Cambridge: Harvard University Press, 1973), pp. 80-81.
11. "Questions propounded to the Commissioner of Indian Affairs at meeting held Feby 25/80," Record Group 46, "Records of the U. S. Senate, Committee on Indian Affairs," National Archives, Washington, D.C.
12. Quoted in Prucha, *Americanizing the American Indians*, pp. 83-86.
13. Helen H. Jackson to Henry W. Longfellow, March 10, 1881; Jackson to Holmes, March 2, 1881, Jackson papers, Houghton Library, Harvard University, Cambridge, Mass.
14. Helen Hunt Jackson, *A Century of Dishonor* (New York: Harper & Brothers, 1881), p. 30; George W. Manypenny, *Our Indian Wards*, ed. Henry E. Fritz (New York: Da Capo Press, 1972).
15. Wilcomb E. Washburn, ed., *The American Indian and the United States: A Documentary History*, 4 vols. (New York: Random House, 1973), p. 1720.
16. *The Council Fire* 2, no. 2 (February, 1879).
17. The Curtis Act is reprinted in Washburn, *American Indian and the United States*, pp. 2194-2208; remarks of President Cleveland quoted in Everett Arthur Gilcreast, "Richard Henry Pratt and American Indian Policy, 1877-1906: A Study of the Assimilation Movement," Ph.D. Dissertation, Yale University, 1967, pp. 213-14.
18. Washburn, *American Indian and the United States*, p. 1697; Prucha, *Americanizing the American Indian*, p. 134.
19. Washburn, *American Indian and the United States*, p. 1704.
20. Lewis H. Morgan, *Houses and House-Life of the American Aborigines* ed. Paul Bohannan (Chicago: University of Chicago Press, 1965), pp. 80-81.
21. Washburn, *American Indian and the United States*, pp. 1686, 1714, 1718-19, 1748-49.
22. Ibid., pp. 1752-54.
23. *The Council Fire* 4, no. 2 (February 1881): 19-22.
24. Ibid., 3, no. 5 (May 1, 1880): 67.
25. Alice C. Fletcher and Francis La Flesche, "The Omaha Tribe," Smithsonian Institution, Bureau of American Ethnology, *Annual Report*, vol. 27 (Washington: 1905-1906 [actually published in 1911]), pp. 636-37; U.S., Congress, Senate, Committee on Indian Affairs, *Memorial of the Members of the Omaha Tribe of Indians for a Grant of Land in Severalty*, 47th Cong., 1st sess., Misc. Doc. No. 31, Jan. 11, 1882.
26. U.S., Congress, House, *Report to Accompany Bill S. 1255, on Sale of a Part of Omaha Indian Reservation in Nebraska, July 1, 1882, 47th Cong., 1st sess. H. Rep. 1530*; also Alice C. Fletcher, *Historical Sketch of the Omaha Tribe of Indians in Nebraska* (Washington, 1885), p. 8.
27. *Proceedings of the Fourth Annual Lake Mohonk Conference, October 12, 13, 14, 1886* (Philadelphia, 1887), p. 8; Nancy Oestreich Lurie, "Women in Early American Anthropology," in *Pioneers of American Anthropology: The Uses of Biography*, ed. June Helm (Seattle: University of Washington Press, 1966), pp. 52-53.
28. Loring Benson Priest, *Uncle Sam's Stepchildren: The Reformation of United States Indian Policy* (New Brunswick, N.J.: Rutgers University Press, 1942), pp. 194-95.
29. *Second Annual Address to the Public of the Lake Mohonk Conference held at Lake Mohonk, N.Y., September, 1884, in Behalf of the Civilization and Legal Protection of the Indians of the United States* (Philadephia, 1884), pp. 5-6.
30. Ibid., pp. 7-13, 25-26.

2
The Decision for Compulsory Allotment of Land

Severalty bills continued to be introduced, discussed in committees, and favorably reported in successive Congresses but without any final disposition. Representatives of the Indian Rights Association fed Senator Dawes and others suggested modifications of the severalty bill, as, for example, a provision to force the immediate extension of law over the Indians, without waiting for the completion of allotment as specified in the Coke bill.[1]

It soon became apparent that one of the sticking points was the first section of the bill, which authorized the president to issue patents for Indian reservations in favor of the several *tribes* holding them. Under these patents, the United States was to hold the patented land in trust for the several tribes for twenty-five years, and at the end of that time convey it by patent to the different tribes clear of encumbrance. The purpose of this provision was to secure the tribes as such in the possession of their reservations. As the Indian Rights Association put it in its discussion of the Coke bill in 1884 (see Document 4), "It places the strong restraint of the law upon the unjust occupation of Indian lands in the incessant push of Western settlement." The bill went on to provide for allotting tribal lands in severalty to Indian individuals, but the act as a whole would not apply to tribes as such until the consent of two-thirds of the adult male members of the tribe had been obtained.[2]

The stage was thus set for the climactic debate which took place not in the halls of Congress, but at the resort hotel at Lake Mohonk where the Indian reformers gathered in October of 1885. Preparations for the 1885 Lake Mohonk meeting mark the turning point in the debate over Indian severalty, for it was at this time that the resort to coercion and involuntary means to achieve severalty were proposed and, by skillful management, agreed upon by the varied forces seeking solution of the Indian problem (*Alternative 4*). The policy recommendations adopted at Lake Mohonk in October 1885 were initially put forward during an informal meeting held in the offices of the *Christian Union*, in New York City, on July 7, at the instigation of its editor, the Reverend Dr. Lyman Abbott (see Document 5). That meeting expressed Dr. Abbott's coercive, "hard-line" views and, while acknowledging the objections or qualifications of individuals like Alice Fletcher and founder of the Carlisle Indian Industrial School Captain Richard H. Pratt, outlined a policy that was carried successfully in the formal Mohonk meeting a few months later, and, eventually, in the bill that bore Senator Dawes's name.[3]

The results of the New York meeting were conveyed to Senator Dawes by Abbott, in a letter of July 20, 1885 (see Document 6) which outlined in clear detail the policy advocated by the hardliners.

"The Reservation Must Go"

Abbott, who cheerfully admitted in his *Reminiscences* (Boston, 1915), published near the end of his life, that he had never visited an Indian reservation or known more than ten Indians, took pride in the role of his journal in shaping public opinion on the Indian question. As early as 1879 the *Christian Union* (later *The Outlook*) had urged abandonment of the tribal system. In the issue of June 11, 1885, Abbott had included a short paragraph urging the abolition of Indian reservations. In the issue of July 16, 1885, one week after the meeting in his office, Abbott headlined the proposed new policy in a forceful editorial entitled "The Reservation Must Go." In a striking phrase, Abbott asserted that "barbarism has no rights which civilization is bound to respect," a position which he also conveyed to Senator Dawes in personal correspondence prior to the Lake Mohonk Conference.[4]

So blatant was Abbott's attack on the nation's plighted word and so casuistic his rationalizations for ignoring that word that he became an embarrassment to those reformers who were attempting more discreetly to bring the Indian into the American system. Thus Herbert Welsh, of the Indian Rights Association, wrote privately to Dawes attributing Abbott's position to his enthusiasm and ignorance of the true facts. Welsh hoped that exposure to the facts would correct his views. At the same time, Welsh published a response to Abbott's *Christian Union* articles deploring their advocacy of a destruction of Indian treaties as a first step toward solving the Indian problem. Abbott, in response to Welsh's views, persisted in his belief that "barbarism has no rights which civilization is bound to respect."

> Our first duty to the Indians is to give them the benefit of that civilization which we enjoy. They are in fact part of our commonwealth, subject to our authority, amenable to our law. They are no longer a foreign people and cannot be treated as such. . . . We reply that such treaty obligations themselves violate the superior law of civilization, that a treaty which devotes a land to idleness and a people to barbarism cannot stand.[5]

Totally undaunted by his own ignorance or the expressed opposition of men like Welsh and Dawes, Abbott "began at once an editorial agitation for the abandonment of the reservation system as preliminary to the introduction of this revolutionary conception at the next Lake Mohonk Conference." Powerful editorials headed "Justice, Not Charity, for the Indian" and "What to Do with Lo" attacked earlier solutions, including the Coke bill, which had hitherto expressed the reformers' position.[6]

The debate over the policy of coercion (*Alternative 4*) at Lake Mohonk was spirited. General S. C. Armstrong, principal of the Hampton Normal School, which played a leading role in educating Indians as well as blacks, fully supported the proposition presented for the consideration of the conference that, if the consent of a tribe to allotment could not be obtained, then it should be carried out without tribal consent. Armstrong, his words foreshadowing a later justification for saving a Vietnamese town by destroying it, explained that though coercion might seem harsh, "it is done with a feeling that we must save them from themselves." Armstrong also evoked "the spirit of the country—of its inevitable growth" as an explanation of why the Indian had to be forced to change.[7]

Dr. Abbott, consistent with his previously expressed views, was equally insistent that nothing—even treaty obligations—should be allowed to stand in the way of the reformers' commitment to do good to the Indians.[8]

Senator Henry L. Dawes, steeled by Herbert Welsh to oppose the Abbott position, spoke against forced allotment. The opportunity to take land in severalty, Dawes asserted, "must be the Indian's choice." Dawes ridiculed the idea that "you can take an Indian against his will—by the nape of his neck, if I may say so—tell him to be a farmer and then go off and leave him...." Dawes opposed the instant abolition of reservations. The civilization of the Indian "is a work of time" and at this stage Dawes was prepared to allow the Indian that time.[9]

Dawes was particularly outraged at the loose talk about breaking up Indian reservations in violation of existing treaties and title. To talk of taking land from the Indians without their consent "for their good," Dawes insisted, "is the same as talking about taking away our neighbor's title to his home for his good." How would you, Dawes asked the delegates, "like to have your town vote that it would be for your good to move somewhere else, and they take your home?" Dawes reminded his audience how recently friends of the Indian, such as the Woman's National Indian Association, had petitioned Congress to uphold its treaty obligations to the Indians. He begged them not to pressure members of Congress who had responded to earlier pleas to uphold Indian treaty rights, to "openly violate the solemn treaties they have made."[10]

Yet Senator Dawes, for all his concern for easing the Indian gently into equal citizenship, could not perceive that the existence of land in common might have some redeeming feature.

> It is Henry George's system, and under that there is no enterprise to make your home any better than that of your neighbors. There is no selfishness, which is at the bottom of civilization. Till this people will consent to give up their lands, and divide them among their citizens so that each can own the land he cultivates they will not make much more progress.[11]

Colonel William McMichael, of the Board of Indian Commissioners, in discussing the Indians of the Indian Territory, responded, with perhaps some irony:

They have schools, a representative government, an executive who rules over them. They have a system by which, as I understand, there is no pauper there. And what is it that they do *not* have? Why, they do not have the avarice and the selfishness which are necessary to the acquisition of private property.

McMichael also rejected Armstrong's coercive benevolence. "[W]e must protect the Indian," he noted, "not against himself, but against ourselves."[12]

John H. Oberly, superintendent of Indian Schools, also protested the proposals of Abbott and Armstrong to ignore the treaty rights of the Indians and to compel them to accept severalty. Oberly conceded the value of admitting the Indian to American citizenship, destroying the reservation system, allotting lands in severalty, and compelling Indians to work: the program advocated by the reformers. But, he insisted, the order should be reversed.

I would first teach the Indian how to work; then I would teach him our ideas of the rights of property, and give him lands in severalty; then I would abolish the reservation system; and then make the Indian a citizen and enfranchize him.

Oberly would prepare him by thorough education to assume the responsibilities the others wished to thrust upon him.[13]

The platform, as finally approved by the 1885 Lake Mohonk Conference, was sufficiently ambiguous to be acceptable to both pro- and anti-coercionists. The conference agreed that in order to implement its recommendations on breaking up communal land holdings and providing land in severalty to Indians, "negotiations should be entered into for the modification of the present treaties, and these negotiations should be pressed in every honorable way until the consent of the Indians be obtained."[14]

While Mrs. Dawes deluded herself with the idea that her husband, during the Mohonk conference, had "smashed" Dr. Abbott, in fact Dawes came soon to accept the coercive views of the determined editor. As Abbott later put it with quiet irony:

Senator Dawes, of Massachusetts, one of the best friends the Indian ever had, devoted an evening to an eloquent address in condemnation of this policy [recommended by Abbott]. Two years after he introduced into the United States Senate a bill for putting the policy into effect; it is known in history as the 'Dawes Bill.'[15]

Indian "Benefits" and White Interests

The inconsistency and even hypocrisy of the Lake Mohonk recommendations in 1885 were pointed out in the November 1885 issue of the *Council Fire* in an editorial statement (see Document 7), and by former commissioner of Indian Affairs, George W. Manypenny, in a letter to the journal (see Document 8). Manypenny noted that Dr. James E. Rhoads, (president of the business committee of the Friends of the Indians), in his introductory speech before the conference, had declared that the Indian question could never be settled except upon the principles of justice and equal rights. Yet he had gone on to urge the abrogation of the reservation system, the dissolution of the tribal relation, and the subjection of the Indian as a citizen to the law. To accomplish these ends, Manypenny noted, Rhoads had recommended negotiation with the Indian tribes to obtain their consent to these measures, but, failing to obtain such consent, then execution without their consent. Manypenny recalled his own role in negotiating agreements with some of the tribes west of Missouri for the extinguishment of the title to their lands in the early 1850s. Manypenny had believed that good results would follow from the treaties he made, but had since realized he was wrong.[16]

The potency of the theoretical assumption of the desirability of allotment over the practical evidence of its effect is perhaps nowhere better demonstrated than in the response of the forty-nine Indian agents whose advice on the desirability of allotment had been solicited by the Board of Indian Commissioners in November 1885. Not a single agent believed the Indians under his charge were ready for allotment, and more than half doubted that the policy could succeed.[17]

The reformers were well aware of the need to tie their reforms to the white man's interest, but hoped that, in the process, both would benefit (*Alternative 5: Benefits to the white man*). Professor C. C. Painter, at the 1885 Lake Mohonk Conference, had described the frustrations of a Washington lobbyist for the Indian cause: endless delays; endless referrals; endless red tape. "If you are working for any legislation in the direction of the Indian you will find," Painter noted, that "unless you can identify it with the white interest so that that will carry it, that you are tied." Painter's reaction to the frustration was typical of the reformers. "I am satisfied that the time has come when we should sweep this whole system away and put the Indian on the basis of a white man, and give him a man's chance to this country under the law."[18]

Lucius Quintus Cincinnatus Lamar of Mississippi, secretary of the interior in the cabinet of President Cleveland from 1885 until 1888, observed to Senator Dawes in a letter of November 13, 1885, shortly after the conclusion of the Lake Mohonk Conference, that some of the proposed solutions to the Indian problem were "dictated less by a regard for the interests of the Indian than for those of the white people who want his lands."

> It would solve the problem very quickly to set him free from reservations, tribal relations, and the supervision of the government. It would hurt no interest in this country to do so, but it would, by destroying the Indians, violate the moral obligation under which this nation rests to protect the Indians, to ameliorate their condition, and to spare no effort nor expense nor sacrifice to elevate them to a position fitting them to be citizens of the United States.[19]

The temper underlying the humanitarianism of the reformers was shown in their support of Senator Dawes's Sioux bill, which proposed to divide the reservation of the Sioux Nation into separate reservations and to secure the relinquishment of Indian title to the remainder. The Indian Rights Association, in supporting the bill in a statement of February 23, 1886, noted how the Great Sioux Reservation blocked the path of settlers and railroads. "*We cannot stop the legitimate advance of emigration and civilization if we would,*" the statement noted, "*and, we add most emphatically, we would not if we could;* . . ." The association, however, wished that the process could be done with Indian consent, and that the surplus derived from the sale of the excess lands be used to help the Indians.[20]

The probable role of railroad corporations in promoting severalty legislation has been frequently alluded to, but little evidence exists to connect railroads and the promoters of the bill. D. S. Otis, author of a history of the Dawes Act and the allotment of Indian lands published in 1934, wrote that he had been "unable to discover any explicit expression of a railroad's attitude toward the passage of the general allotment act." Yet he noted that the same Congress that passed the Dawes Act "went in for grants of railroad rights-of-way through Indian lands on a new and enlarged scale." Of the nine Indian bills that became law in that session, six, Otis pointed out, were grants to railroads. Moreover, in the session following that in which the Dawes Act was passed—the first session of the Fiftieth Congress—thirteen laws were passed which granted railroads rights-of-way through Indian territories; while in the second session of the same Congress, ten such laws were passed.[21]

The wording of Section 10 of the Dawes Act confirms the suspicion that railroads were acutely conscious of their interests in severalty legislation (see Document 9). Section 10 explicitly disclaims any interference with the right and power of Congress to grant rights-of-way through any lands granted to an Indian, or to a tribe of Indians, for railroad or highway purposes "for the public use" and specifically provides for the power of condemnation upon making just compensation."[22] Congress continued to provide railroad rights-of-way in subsequent years, authorizing a high of fifteen such grants in 1898.[23]

The questionable character of railroad activity in the late 1880s is indicated by the comment of President Grover Cleveland, in his fourth annual message in 1888, concerning the multiplying "grants of doubtful expediency to railroad corporations, permitting them to pass through Indian reservations, . . ."[24]

Although it may be argued that obtaining rights-of-way from many individual Indian allottees would be harder than obtaining such rights from a few tribal leaders, the evidence suggests that neither approach posed great difficulties for railroad corporations. Tribal leaders were perhaps more sensitive to the worth of the rights being asked for and more reluctant to concede them than individual Indians who could be easily seduced or overridden. Nevertheless, under either method railroad construction marched successfully forward. Under allotment, the railroads had the added benefit of an expected rapid increase in white settlement along the proposed lines, a growth which would not have taken place had tribal holdings remained intact.

The Council Fire, in an article printed in its June 1885 issue, asserted that allotment was neither for the benefit of the Indians nor of the people of the United States, but for the benefit of railroad corporations, "who, as soon as the present title is extinguished, are to have 23,800,000 acres of the Indian lands." The United States had promised by treaty that tribes should have patents to the lands they retained in exchange for the lands they gave up. "This is too long for railroads to wait, hence this present title must be destroyed by having the Congress of the United States to allot in severalty to the Indians and give them a better title...."[25]

Philanthropists viewed the influence of the railroad with equanimity or even with favor. Some regarded its progress as inevitable and its power as irresistible. Dr. Lyman Abbott asserted that the railroad "with all its corruptions, is a Christianizing power, and will do more to teach the people punctuality than schoolmaster or preacher can."[26]

In sum, it seems evident that the railroads stood to obtain their needed rights-of-way whether or not tribal lands were allotted. They did not need to lobby extensively for or against the allotment bill. They could rely on others to promote their ends: eastern philanthropists, western landseekers, and other interested parties. Undoubtedly they saw severalty as facilitating their ultimate ends, but saw no need to expose their special interests too openly.

The "Inevitable" Breakup of the Reservations

The pressures for opening up the reservations came not only from humanitarians and landgrabbers but from agencies like the United States Army. Lieutenant General Philip H. Sheridan, in his *Annual Report of the Lieutenant General of the Army*, (Washington, October 10, 1886), repeated his recommendation of the previous year that each Indian family be located upon an individual settlement and the remainder of each reservation be sold, the proceeds of which sale to be used to support the Indians. Sheridan noted that:

> The Indian reservations of the United States contain about 200,000 square miles, and their population is about 260,000. Twenty-six thousand square miles would locate each family upon a half section of land, leaving a surplus of about 170,000 square miles, which, according to the plan I have proposed, would produce annually $4,480,000. This amount exceeds by about $660,000 the entire sum appropriated for the payment of their annuities and for their subsistence and civilization.[27]

White farmers, speculators, railroad men, and frontiersmen generally resented the Coke bill's guarantee of tribal land as inalienable for twenty-five years and Congress had, as noted earlier, held back from passage of such a bill. When the humanitarians concluded that the guarantee of tribal land should be eliminated in order to get an allotment bill, the "restraint" upon the "unjust occupation of Indian lands in the incessant push of Western settlement," which the Indian Rights Association had talked about in 1884, was effectively destroyed. At this critical juncture, in February of 1886, Senator Henry Dawes introduced a new allotment bill in the Senate which differed from the Coke bill only in a provision to allow the secretary of the interior to purchase any portion of an Indian reservation not needed for allotment. The bill, as one authority has noted, passed the Senate in "record time."[28]

The process by which Senator Dawes was gradually converted to a more coercive bill (*Alternative 4*) was outlined by himself during the Fourth Lake Mohonk Conference in 1886. The bill to which his name was now attached, he noted, originated with Secretary of the Interior Carl Schurz (1877-1881) and Senator Samuel J. Kirkwood, Republican of Iowa, 1877-1881, who succeeded Schurz as secretary of the interior for the period of Garfield's presidency. It had then gone to the Committee on Indian Affairs of the Senate and finally emerged as the Coke bill. Although at first insisting on the sanctity of the tribal patent and the government's treaty obligations, Dawes found himself in a continuing fight with "Western men who are bent upon taking land from these Indians without the slightest regard to their rights or the obligations the Government had entered into." At first, Dawes noted, he attempted to guarantee to the tribes the security of their reservations. But

> Every year I have been weakening on it because I have come, from year to year, to the conclusion that this pressure upon the Indian for his lands has come to be irresistible, and that we have got to make provision for him now just as quick as we can, or we shall lose the opportunity. I have come to the conclusion that the quicker he is mingled with the whites in every particular the better it will be.

Similarly, in regard to the Sioux bill to reduce the Great Sioux Reservation to remnants of its former greatness, which Dawes also sponsored, he confessed:

> I became satisfied—no man can go there and not be satisfied—that those white men will have a large portion of that reservation; that this land cannot be kept by Indians with a population increasing all around them. I made up my mind that I could do more good by accepting the inevitable, and seeing to it that if they part with their land they shall have an equivalent for it. Out of that has come this bill, and if anybody is alarmed, let him rest upon this section which requires a vote of approval of three-fourths of the Indians.[29]

Thus we have the remarkable confession of the philanthropic senator from Massachusetts that he dared not combat the greedy landgrabbers but preferred to bow to the "inevitable," seeing to it only that the Indians received at least some consideration for the sacrifice that he would offer in their name. Even though doubts assailed him prior to the passage of the act, and even more so after the passage of the act, Dawes perceived his role as a statesmanlike one.[30]

Allotment and Citizenship: "Adopting the Habits of Civilized Life"

Although land in severalty was the key plank in the reform plan, subsidiary issues forced their way into the package that eventually became the Dawes Act. While the land allotment measures were the principal method of separating the individual Indian from his tribal heritage, the application of American citizenship (as well as American law) to the Indian affected by allotment seemed to some a necessary concomitant. Yet opinion was divided, legally, morally, and practically. Despite the symbolic aura of American citizenship as marking final acceptance of the Indian into the American body politic, the "gift" was two-sided. Not only did it subject the Indian to the responsibilities as well as the privileges of the citizen, but it made the less sophisticated Indian citizen easier prey to his more calculating and experienced white citizen neighbor. Hence opponents and proponents of citizenship as a corollary of the severalty bill argued long and heatedly about its wisdon.

What tipped the scales in favor of including a citizenship provision in the bill was the case of *John Elk v. Charles Wilkins* in 1884. Elk, an Indian who had voluntarily separated himself from his tribe and taken up residence among the white citizens of Nebraska, was denied the right to register to vote, although he met all the apparent qualifications of a voter, by Wilkins, registrar in the fifth ward of the city of Omaha, on the grounds that he was not a citizen of the United States. The Supreme Court upheld the decision of the local court, although two justices dissented, asserting that the Court's decision meant that "there is still in this country a despised and rejected class of persons, with no nationality whatever; who, born in our territory, owing no allegiance to any foreign power, and subject as residents of the States to all the burdens of government, are yet not members of any political community nor entitled to any of the rights, privileges, or immunities of citizens of the United States."[31]

Senator Dawes also disagreed with the Court's ruling and compared it in wickedness to the pre-Civil War decisions in the fugitive slave cases. The Court, in its decision, had thrown the question of determining the citizenship status of the Indian directly to Congress. Reformers immediately took up the cue and debated the form in which citizenship should be legislated for the Indian. The apparent inequity and absurdity of the ruling struck the logical and idealistic minds of the Indian reformers with great force. The pathos was compounded by letters such as that which Senator Dawes received from "Bright Eyes," the educated Indian wife of the Omaha newspaperman and champion of the Poncas, Thomas H. Tibbles. Bright Eyes wrote: "I see that the Supreme Court has decided that the Indian is not a citizen. What can be done about it? Would a bill have to be brought in Congress making the Indians citizens?"[32]

The effect of *Elk v. Wilkins* was to spur the reformers to insert a provision in the bill (Section 6) which provided that every Indian born within the territorial limits of the United States "to whom allotments shall have been made under the provisions of this act, or under any law or treaty, and every Indian born within the territorial limits of the United States who has voluntarily taken up, within said limits, his residence separate and apart from any tribe of Indians therein, and has adopted the habits of civilized life, is hereby declared to be a citizen of the United States, . . ." (see Document 9).

Prior to 1884 there had been general agreement that education of the Indian should precede all other reforms. Secretary of the Interior Henry Teller had put it most succinctly in a speech at Carlisle Indian School in 1883: "Education, preparation, first; lands in severalty and citizenship afterward." There was also a widespread belief in the advantages of boarding school education for the Indian. With the rush toward citizenship and land in severalty, however, the priorities were reversed. "In place of the theory that the Indian must be trained for citizenship and land ownership appeared the idea that the exercise of citizenship would train the Indian." A new emphasis was placed on day schools. Elaine Goodale's tract on the subject, published by the Indian Rights Association in 1886, attacked eastern schools because they separated parent from child. The new theory was that the children educated at the day schools would educate their parents directly.[33]

Towards a Coercive Stance

The paradox of reformers and humanitarians, who had vigorously opposed forcible removal of Indians, finally brought to demand forcible allotment of their lands and destruction of their tribal organization, did not escape the notice and criticism of those who argued for Indian consent. It is more difficult to explain why the humanitarians suddenly changed their views.[34]

Dawes's ability to compromise, even with principle, was true to his character. When he first came to Washington in 1852 and attended the Republican Convention in Baltimore shortly thereafter, he confided in his diary that he had voted to nominate General Winfield Scott and for the platform even though it "contained principles, which I did not approve." "I have tried to school myself to feel that the end justified it," Dawes went on, "and I may be able so to do. . . . It was a departure from a rule of action to do what in itself is right and leave the consequence to God, for which I hope I shall be able to find a justification." Dawes's good New England character is revealed in one of the following entries, that for January 3, 1876, which notes that, despite a firm resolve to continue writing daily in his diary, which he had made in 1853, "This resolution I kept as it appears for *two* days!" "This is a fair specimen of the resolutions of my life," Dawes went on. "I make good ones enough but keep few of them."[35]

The final passage of the Dawes Act—which proved something of an anticlimax—reflected the careful planning that preceded it and the flexible character of Senator Dawes. The Senate passed the bill proposed by Dawes on February 25, 1886, after a brief debate. The bill authorized the president to break up Indian reservations, allot to the Indians from 40 to 160 acres of their own lands, and open the remainder to white settlement without consultation with the affected Indians. The Indian Committee of the House of Representatives, in response to the protest of the National Indian Defence Association, an organization reflecting the views of Dr. T. A. Bland, editor of the *Council Fire* and general agent of the association, secured the adoption of an amendment in the House version, approved December 15, 1886, which made it impossible for the president to break up a reservation without the consent of a majority of the adult male Indians. However, the stay of execution was brief. A conference committee of the two houses eliminated the House provision for Indian consent and the conference committee report was accepted by the House on January 21, 1887. The Senate approved the final version, and the bill was signed into law by President Grover Cleveland on February 8, 1887. Not once was a record vote taken on a subject relating to the bill.[36] Lyman Abbott's *Christian Union*, in its July 7, 1887, issue noted proudly that, "The definite policy, first formulated in the editorial rooms of The Christian Union, then adopted by the Conference at Lake Mohonk, has been accepted by the country, by the Administration, by Congress."[37]

The ease with which Dawes was able to surmount his distaste for the coercive measures advocated by Abbott, with their implicit repudiation of the nation's plighted word incorporated in earlier treaties, is perhaps explicable in terms of Dawes's emotional reaction to the frustration of the moment but it may more readily be explained by his long standing conviction that the Indian treaty system was an anomaly within the American commonwealth. While chairman of the Appropriations Committee of the House sixteen years earlier, Dawes had almost single-handedly forced the Senate to do away with the treaty system as the price for obtaining appropriations from the House for carrying out the government's commitments to the Indian. As one scholar has put it, "Dawes, refusing to acknowledge an Indian treaty in the full constitutional sense of the word, claimed for the House the right to refuse to make appropriations for their execution, while the Senate held fast to its treaty-making power and resented the refusal of the House to provide appropriations for them." Although the amendment to an appropriations bill in 1871, providing that no more treaties would be made with Indians, is usually interpreted as a simple compromise between a jealous House and a reluctant Senate over participation in the making of Indian policy, in fact Dawes consistently asserted in congressional debates that his real concern was to break up the treaty system as the first step toward general allotment of Indian lands. Thus his success in 1871 in obtaining the abandonment of the treaty system, and a House role in all subsequent Indian legislation, can be interpreted as a fundamental step toward allotment.[38]

The passage of the Dawes Act did not still the controversy over allotment of land in severalty. Dr. T. A. Bland threw a scare into the proponents of the legislation by preparing to contest its constitutionality. A letter from Thomas A. Tibbles, the Ponca champion, to Senator Dawes, March 16, 1887, warned the senator that the "Bland people" would seek to overturn the act on the grounds that "treaty titles to the land give them a vested interest, and that Congress cannot legislate concerning this, without the consent of the Indians, not even to change it from a tribal title to an individual title."[39]

The Indian Rights Association in May rushed to the defense of the Dawes Act with a reprint of an attack on Bland and the Indian Defense Association, which appeared in the *Boston Post*, April 6, 1887.[40]

Bland's attack, however, proved abortive and the humanitarians vied with each other in claiming credit for the act. In *A Brief Statement of the Objects, Achievements and Needs of the Indian Rights Association*, published in Philadelphia in 1887, the association, ignoring the role of Abbott and the

Lake Mohonk conference organizers, asserted that

The law providing for the allotment of lands in severalty to Indians, which was passed last winter, was devised and prepared in accordance and cooperation with the plans and objects of the Association, and its passage was the result, as even the enemies of the measure affirmed, of the efforts of the Association in placing the entire subject in the clear light of facts, and thus convincing members of Congress and their constituents that justice to the Indians and the interests of white people of the country alike demanded the passage of the 'Dawes Bill.' The Association accepts the responsibility for the enactment of this law, and also the strenuous obligation to assist in its honest and faithful application in the interests of the Indians.[41]

Notes

1. Henry S. Pancoast to Henry L. Dawes, November 22, 1884, Dawes Papers, General Correspondence, Box 26, Library of Congress, Washington, D.C.
2. Henry S. Pancoast, *Indian Land in Severalty as Provided for by the Coke Bill, Forty-eighth Congress, First Session, S. 48* (Philadelphia, 1884), p. 4.
3. Dawes Papers, General Correspondence, Box 27.
4. Lyman Abbott to Henry L. Dawes, July 20, 1885, Dawes Papers, quoted in Loring Benson Priest, *Uncle Sam's Stepchildren: The Reformation of United States Indian Policy* (New Brunswick, N.J.: Rutgers University Press, 1942), p. 244.
5. Herbert Welsh to Henry L. Dawes, July 25, 1885, Dawes Papers, Box 27; Ibid., Box 63, Scrapbook, 1885.
6. Lyman Abbott, *Reminiscences* (Boston: Houghton Mifflin Co., 1915), p. 427; *The Christian Union* 32, no. 4 (July 23, 1885): 3; 32, no. 5 (July 30, 1885): 4-5.
7. *Proceedings of the Third Annual Meeting of the Lake Mohonk Conference of Friends of the Indian, Held October 7 to 9, 1885* (Philadelphia, 1886), p. 28.
8. Ibid., pp. 50-54.
9. Ibid., p. 39.
10. Ibid., pp. 40-41, 47.
11. Ibid., p. 43.
12. Ibid., p. 67.
13. Ibid., p. 58.
14. Ibid., p. 49.
15. Mrs. Dawes to daughter Anna, October 11, 1885, Dawes Papers, General Correspondence, Box 27; Abbott, *Reminiscences*, p. 428.
16. *The Council Fire* 8, no. 11.
17. Priest, *Uncle Sam's Stepchildren*, p. 236, based on letters received by the Board of Indian Commissioners, National Archives, Washington, D.C.
18. *Proceedings of the Third Annual Meeting of the Lake Mohonk Conference*, p. 14.
19. Dawes Papers, General Correspondence, Box 27, quoted in Ira V. Brown, *Lyman Abbott: Christian Evolutionalist, A Study in Religious Liberalism* (Cambridge: Harvard University Press, 1953), p. 95.
20. Indian Rights Association, *Popular statement and abstract of "An Act to divide a portion of the reservation of the Sioux Nation of Indians, in Dakota, into Separate Reservations..."* (Philadelphia, 1886), pp. 1-7, at p. 2.
21. Delos Sacket Otis, *The Dawes Act and the Allotment of Indian Lands*, ed. Francis Paul Prucha (Norman: University of Oklahoma Press, 1973), pp. 23-24.
22. Ibid., p. 24.
23. Ibid., p. 25.
24. Quoted in ibid., p. 27.

25. Quoted from *Indian Missionary*, McAllester, Indian Territory, which paper quoted it from the *Buckner College Journal*. "We recognize the initials as those of our esteemed friend Major Isaac G. Vore, who has spent almost his entire life in the Indian Territory, and was for many years clerk of Union agency, at Muskogee." (Bland's note).
26. Quoted in Otis, *The Dawes Act*, pp. 29-30.
27. Printed document in Miscellaneous Documents Relating to Indian Affairs, Department of the Interior Library, pp. 11651-63.
28. Robert Winston Mardock, *The Reformers and the American Indian* (Columbia: University of Missouri Press, 1971), p. 216.
29. *Proceedings of the Fourth Annual Lake Mohonk Conference, October 12, 13, 14, 1886* (Philadelphia, 1887), p. 31, 33-34; *Proceedings of the Third Annual Meeting*, p. 38.
30. *Proceedings of the Fourth Annual Conference*, p. 33, where Dawes notes that, "A few years ago we were enchanted with that absurd idea" that the Indian could be forced to take land in severalty. See also the *Proceedings of the Fifth Annual Meeting of the Lake Mohonk Conference of Friends of the Indian. Held Sept. 28 to 30, 1887* (Philadelphia, 1887), pp. 68-69, where Dawes notes that "the greed of these people for the land has made it utterly impossible to preserve it for the Indian."
31. 112 U.S. 94, reprinted in Wilcomb E. Washburn, ed., *The American Indian and the United States*, 4 vols. (New York: Random House, 1973), p. 1720.
32. Bright Eyes to Henry L. Dawes, November 12, 1884, Dawes Papers, General Correspondence, Box 26; Priest, *Uncle Sam's Stepchildren*, p. 207.
33. Quoted in *The Council Fire*, June, 1883, and in Everett Arthur Gilcreast, "Richard Henry Pratt and American Indian Policy, 1877-1906: A Study of the Assimilation Movement," Ph.D. Dissertation, Yale University, 1967, pp. 195-96.
34. Priest, *Uncle Sam's Stepchildren*, p. 238.
35. Dawes Papers, Letterbook marked "Letters," but containing diary entries beginning March 23, 1852, entry for June 27, pp. 34-35.
36. *The Council Fire* 9, no. 11-12 (November-December, 1886): 158; Priest, *Uncle Sam's Stepchildren*, p. 187; Samuel Taylor, "The Origins of the Dawes Act of 1887," Philip Washburn Prize Thesis, Harvard University, 1927, pp. 61-62.
37. *The Christian Union* 36: 2-3; quoted in Ira Brown, *op. cit.*, p. 95.
38. Fred H. Nicklason, "The Early Career of Henry L. Dawes, 1816-1871," Ph.D. Dissertation, Yale University, 1967, p. 369; Priest, *Uncle Sam's Stepchildren*, pp. 95-102.
39. Dawes Papers, General Correspondence, Box 28.
40. Indian Rights Association, *Allotment of Lands: Defense of the Dawes Indian Severalty Bill* (Philadelphia, 1887), pp. 1-5.
41. *A Brief Statement of the Objects, Achievements and Needs of the Indian Rights Association* (Philadelphia, 1887), p. 5.

Epilogue
Impact of the Decision

Indian Losses, White Gains

The self-righteousness of the reformers continued to blind them to the facts, even when it became evident that the Dawes Act was not working. Philanthropists like James B. Thayer, in an article entitled "A People Without Law" in the *Atlantic Monthly* issue of October, 1891, insisted that the crying need was instant legislation to subject the Indian to United States law. Senator Dawes, in a bitter response at the Lake Mohonk Conference in 1891, rejected categorically the assertion that the Indians were without law, pointing out the provisions in the Dawes Act itself, those in the Major Crimes Act of 1885, as well as the Courts of Indian Offenses authorized under Department of the Interior regulations, the operation of which Dawes compared favorably with the functioning of U.S. courts.

Yet the mentality which could demand absolute, rigorous, and unbending adherence to a cultural ideal totally alien to the people being subjected to it was also the mentality that would doggedly and righteously lobby in Congress and in the meeting houses and pulpits of America for such changes. The occasional expressions of opposition to such culturally insensitive policies lacked the same organization, same moral authority, and same dogged determination that the reformers possessed.

A measure of the naiveté of the reformers, especially in their discounting of the extent of concessions to white men in the bill, was their surprise when the American people generally, and those who administered the act in particular, failed to show great concern for helping the Indian adjust to his new circumstances. Although Dawes and the leaders of Indian rights organizations asserted that the act merely provided an *opportunity* to effect a needed change, and required honest administration and increased concern for Indian education and welfare, in fact public interest in and concern for the Indian seriously declined. Membership in Indian rights groups tapered off. Congress showed more concern in the number of acres of Indian land opened to white men than in providing for the education of the red man. In a speech prepared only a few years after the act had become law, Senator Dawes confessed that had the "radical character" of the change made by the allotment act been fully comprehended at the time of its enactment, "it is doubtful if the legislators would then have had the courage to put it on the statute books."[1]

It has been asserted by some students of the subject that the authors of the bill failed to consider the possibility that some Indians would be unable to farm their allotments because of physical disability, age, or other defect, and that provisions to allow them to lease their lands rather than farm them were, as a consequence, inadvertently omitted.[2] In fact, the omission of any provision authorizing leasing derived from the known hostility of the reformers, and particularly Senator Dawes, to the informal practice that had grown up under Department of the Interior regulations of leasing Indian lands to western cattlemen in exchange for payments to the Indians affected. Senator Dawes charged, in a caustic letter to the New York *Tribune* on July 23, 1885, that through such leases Indians like the Cheyennes and Arapahos were enabled to buy Winchester rifles and ammunition in Kansas and to terrorize settlers on the frontier. The relapse of these Indians into their old habits, Dawes noted, was in striking contrast to the situation of Indians where the lease system did not exist. The only positive result of the situation, he believed, was that it would sooner bring about settlement of the Indian question. First, the cattlemen must be controlled.

> Then the Indian must be set upon his own feet on his own homestead, amenable to and protected by the same laws that govern white men. What remains of his lands, not needed for his own actual occupation, should be disposed of to actual homesteaders at the earliest possible date. This done and the Indian problem is solved.[3]

When efforts were made to amend the Dawes Act to incorporate leasing provisions, a purpose finally achieved in the act of February 28, 1891, a number of reformers advocated the measure as a logical extension of the act giving the Indian the right to control his property as he saw fit. Senator Dawes, however, at the 1890 Lake Mohonk Conference, spoke vigorously against the proposal. To accede to the protests against the prohibition based on individual hardships would, he said, threaten "the fundamental idea of the whole system, that controlling idea that work on one's own homestead is the most potent of all civilizing agencies for the Indians." Passage of such a law, Dawes went on, "would speedily overthrow the whole allotment system." Yet characteristically, Dawes had, only a few months before, introduced in the Senate a bill to permit just such leasing authority.[4]

Belated and Halfhearted Regret

It is both simplistic and naive to assert, as did Dawes and as does Loring Benson Priest in his study of the period, that "misapplication by administrators rather than the evil intent of legislators was responsible for the disastrous history of America's first systematic effort to provide for Indian welfare."[5]

It is easier, but no less false, to assert that the Dawes Act was passed because it "had" to be. Certainly the pressures perceived by Senator Dawes and others severely limited the freedom of friends of the Indians to act on their behalf. But what if a man of greater courage and deeper insight than Senator Dawes had taken the leadership? It is a pity that Dawes lacked the inflexible determination of Lyman Abbott or the perceptive insights of

Senator Teller. Had the legislative leadership in the Indian movement coalesced around someone with a different personality, I think the resulting bill might have been able both to provide more guarantees for the Indian future, and fewer plums for voracious white men. Or, it might never have been passed at all. The humanitarians paid too high a price for what they (or rather, the Indians) received, if, indeed, the Indians can be asserted to have received anything. The losses were all on the Indian side; the gains on the white side.

Severalty legislation shattered traditional party lines. Neither political party was strongly identified with the policy. Nor was a western/eastern division the explanation for its passage. The bill was named for an eastern humanitarian. The most effective arguments against severalty were made by a western senator. The bill which eventually passed was a skillful compromise and blending of the interests of land speculators and humanitarians, westerners and easterners, frontiersmen and intellectuals. When the promise of the legislation proved abortive, humanitarians, in the opinion of one historian, sought to blame its failure on "greedy westerners and insensitive administrators rather than their own fantastic expectations."[6]

That the Indians would lose much of their land was expected by the reformers. It was the price that had to be paid for assimilation and admission of the Indian population of the country into the larger body politic with equal rights. But when it became apparent that the Indians had lost not only their "surplus" tribal lands, but (after the expiration of the period of inalienability) their individual allotments to whites better able to compete in the type of society to which Indians had been thrown with inadequate preparation, humanitarians became uncomfortable and embarrassed. Assimilation had obviously not been achieved, and "the Indian problem" remained unsolved. Little wonder that the act soon became a cause for soul-searching.

Professor C. C. Painter, the legislative expert of the Indian Rights Association, readily conceded at the Seventh Annual Meeting of the Lake Mohonk Conference of Friends of the Indian in 1889, that "neither as Christians nor as citizens, can we say with truth to the Indian" what Paul said to the Corinthians: " 'I seek not yours, but you.' " "Even as his friends, and the champions of his cause," Painter went on, "it may be said that we have been more concerned about his property than to secure for him that elevation in character and intelligence which would enable him to take care of it for himself, and that in seeking the lesser we have lost both the greater and the lesser interests."[7]

The regret expressed by those who had sponsored the severalty legislation at the outcome of their handiwork was more formal than real. It was a regret that their plans had gone awry, not that the Indian had been converted from a landed to a landless minority. Moreover, any pain in the aborted outcome of the severalty scheme was eased by the feeling that the continued existence of autonomous tribal entities within the American Union was unthinkable.

It was not until the onset of the Depression, and the reforms of the New Deal in the administration of Franklin D. Roosevelt, that any attempt was made to reverse the tide and correct the injustices flowing from the General Allotment Act. By then it was almost too late. Commissioner of Indian Affairs John Collier's attempts to get already allotted land back into tribal ownership was opposed by increasingly individualistic and acculturated Indians, as well as by many whites. Collier had to settle for half a loaf. Yet the Indian Reorganization Act of 1934 was a frank admission that the United States had made a mistake in 1887, a mistake which it would, thereafter, to the best of its ability, attempt to correct.

Notes

1. Dawes Papers, Speech File "I," Box 47, p. 24, Library of Congress; referred to in Loring Benson Priest, *Uncle Sam's Stepchildren: The Reformation of United States Indian Policy* (New Brunswick, N.J.: Rutgers University Press, 1942), p. 250.
2. Laurence F. Schmeckebier, *The Office of Indian Affairs: Its History, Activities and Organization* (Baltimore: Johns Hopkins Press, 1927), pp. 84, 178.
3. Clipping from the New York *Tribune* in Dawes Papers, Scrapbook, 1885, Box 63.
4. U.S. *Statutes at Large*, vol. 27, pp. 794-96; quoted in Delos Sacket Otis, *The Dawes Act and the Allotment of Indian Lands*, ed. Francis Paul Prucha (Norman: University of Oklahoma Press, 1973), pp. 185-88; Dawes quoted in Otis, *The Dawes Act*, pp. 108-9, 111.
5. Priest, *Uncle Sam's Stepchildren*, p. 250.
6. Everett Arthur Gilcreast, "Richard Henry Pratt and American Indian Policy, 1877-1906: A Study of the Assimilation Movement," Ph.D. Dissertation, Yale University, 1967, pp. 216, 223.
7. Painter's paper on "The Indian and his Property," read on October 3, 1889, *Proceedings of the Seventh Annual Meeting of the Lake Mohonk Conference of Friends of the Indian*, ed. Samuel J. Barrows (Philadelphia, 1889), p. 84.

Part two

Documents of the Decision

1

"The Main Purpose of this Bill Is not to Help the Indian"

On May 28, 1880, the Committee on Indian Affairs of the House of Representatives submitted to the full House a report on H.R. 5038, a bill authorizing the secretary of the interior to allot lands in severalty to Indians. A majority of the committee (six Representatives), after considering whether Congress had the authority to change the provisions of Indian treaties, whether there might not be a better way of accomplishing the purposes of the legislation, and whether the proposed legislation was both expedient and necessary to protect the Indians in the possession of their lands, reported favorably on the bill. Representative Russell Errett, Republican of Pennsylvania, and two other members of the committee submitted a dissenting opinion (*Alternative 2*).

Document†

Views of the Minority

Mr. Errett submitted the following as the views of the minority of the Committee on Indian Affairs:

The undersigned, members of the Committee on Indian Affairs of the House of Representatives, are unable to agree with the majority of the committee in reporting favorably upon this bill, for these, among other, reasons, viz:

1. The bill is confessedly in the nature of an experiment. It is formed solely upon a theory, and it has no practical basis to stand upon. For many

---

†From: U.S., Congress, House, Committee on Indian Affairs, *Lands in Severalty to Indians: Report to Accompany H.R. 5038*, 46th Cong., 2d sess., May 28, 1880, H. Rept. 1576, pp. 7-10.

years it has been the hobby of speculative philanthropists that the true plan to civilize the Indian was to assign him lands in severalty, and thereby make a farmer and self-sustaining citizen of him; and so far back as 1862 Congress established the policy that—

> Whenever any Indian, being a member of any band or tribe with whom the government has or shall have entered into treaty stipulations, being desirous to adopt the habits of civilized life, has had a portion of the lands belonging to his tribe allotted to him in severalty, in pursuance of such treaty stipulations, the agent and superintendent of such tribe shall take such measures, not inconsistent with law, as may be necessary to protect such Indian in the quiet enjoyment of the lands so allotted to him.

This law stands today on the statute book as the recognized policy of this government of the United States in its dealings with the Indians. It does not make allotments of lands in severalty obligatory, but recognizing the plea of those who contend for the beneficent effects sure to flow from the allotment policy, it has opened the door to its establishment, allowing any Indian, in any tribe, desiring to try that policy, a full opportunity to do so under the protection of the government. That law has been upon the statute book for nearly eighteen years, and how many Indians have availed themselves of its provisions? Manifestly, very few; and yet we are told, with great pertinacity, that the Indians are strongly in favor of that policy, and will adopt it if they get a chance. It is surpassing strange, if this be true, that so few have availed themselves of the privileges opened to them by the act of 1862.

Being an experiment merely, it would seem to be the dictate of wisdom to make the trial of putting it into practice on a small basis, say with any one tribe that offers a good opportunity for trying it fairly. The Chippewa bands on Lake Superior, for instance, are alleged to be willing to enter upon the experiment. They have good agricultural lands, are partially civilized and educated, and are sufficiently removed from barbarism to give ground for hope that the experiment may succeed. There could be no very strong reason against trying the experiment merely as an experiment with them. But this bill, without any previous satisfactory test of the policy, proposes to enact a merely speculative theory into a law, and to apply the law to all the Indians, except a few civilized tribes, and to bring them all under its operation without reference to their present condition. It includes the blanket Indians with those who wear the clothing of civilized life; the wild Apaches and Navajos with the nearly civilized Chippewas; and it applies the same rule to all without regard to the wide differences in their condition. It seeks to make a farmer out of the roving and predatory Ute by the same process as would be applied to the nearly civilized Omahas and Poncas. It needs no argument to prove that these Indian tribes vary widely from each other in their civilized attainments, but this bill ignores all these variances as if they did not exist, and erects a Procrustean bed, upon which it would place every Indian, stretching out those who are too short, and cutting off the heads or feet of those who are too long.

It is true that the bill leaves a great deal as to the time of putting the bill in operation to the discretion of the Secretary of the Interior; but we submit that the interests of these tribes are of too great a magnitude to be left to the discretion of any one man, even though he be a Secretary of the Interior. We know of nothing in the constitution of the department that qualifies it peculiarly for such a great trust. Secretaries of the Interior change as frequently as the occurrence of a Mexican of South American revolution; and Congress, we think, is a safer depository for such trusts than any one man, no matter what place he may hold. Let us deal with these people intelligently and wisely, and not at haphazard.

We have said that this bill has no practical basis and is a mere legislative speculation; but it may be added that the experiment it proposes *has* been partially tried, and has always resulted in failure. In the hurry of drawing up reports we cannot be expected to be very specific in our citations, but we may cite the case of the Catawbas, who had lands assigned them in severalty, and who were protected by the inalienability of their homesteads for twenty-five years, just as this bill proposes; and the result was a failure—a flat, miserable failure. The Catawbas gradually withered away under the policy, until there is not one of them left to attest the fact that they ever existed, and their lands fell a prey to the whites who surrounded them and steadily encroached upon them. They were swallowed up as thoroughly as Korah, Dathan and Abiram, when the ground opened beneath their feet and ingulfed them.

II. The plan of this bill is not, in our judgment, the way to civilize the Indian. However much we may differ with the humanitarians who are riding this hobby, we are certain that they will agree with us in the proposition that it does not make a farmer out of an Indian to give him a quarter-section of land. There are hundreds of thousands of white men, rich with the experiences of centuries of Anglo-Saxon civilization who cannot be transformed into cultivators of the land by any such gift. Their habits unfit them for it; and how much more do the habits of the Indian, begotten of hundreds of years of wild life, unfit *him* for entering at once and peremptorily upon a life for which he has no fitness. It requires inclination, agriculture, and training in farming life to make a successful farmer out of even white men, many of whom have failed at the trial of it, even with an inclination for it. How then, is it expected to transform all sorts of Indians, with no fitness or inclination for farming, into successful agriculturists? Surely an act of Congress, however potent in itself, with the addition of the discretion of a Secretary of the Interior, no matter how much of a *doctrinnaire* he may be, are not sufficient to work such a miracle.

The whole training of an Indian from his birth, the whole history of the Indian race, and the entire array of Indian tradition, running back for at least four hundred years, all combine to predispose the Indians against this scheme for his improvement, devised by those who judge him exclusively from *their* standpoint instead of from *his*. From that time of the discovery of America, and for centuries probably before that, the North American Indian has been a communist. Not in the offensive sense of modern communism, but in the sense of holding property in common. The tribal system has kept bands and tribes together as families, each member of which was dependent on the other. The very idea of property in the soil was unknown to the Indian mind. In all the Indian languages there is no word answering to the Latin *habeo*—I have or possess. They had words to denote holding, as "I have a hatchet;" but the idea of the separate possession of property by individuals is as foreign to the Indian mind as communism is to us.

This communistic idea has grown into their very being, and is an integral part of the Indian character. From our point of view this is all wrong; but it is folly to think of uprooting it, strengthened by the traditions of centuries, through the agency of a mere act of Congress, or by the establishment of a theoretical policy. The history of the world shows that it is no easy matter to change old methods of thought or force the adoption of new methods of action. The inborn conservatism of human nature tends always more strongly to the preservation of old ideas than to the establishment of new ones. The world progresses steadily, but always slowly. There are singularities in the Anglo-Saxon character and peculiarities in Anglo-Saxon belief which run back over a thousand years, and which all the enlightenment of progressive centuries has been unable to overcome. There are, even in our own land system, peculiarities which are the remnants of feudal forms and practices, and which still inhere in our methods simply from the force of habit and the conservatism of forms. And if this is true of ourselves, with a written history running back well-nigh two thousand years, why should we be so vain as to expect that the Indian can throw off in a moment, at the bidding of Congress or the Secretary of the Interior, the shackles which have bound his thoughts and action from time immemorial? In this, as in all other cases, it is the dictate of statesmanship to make haste slowly.

We are free to admit that the two civilizations, so different throughout, cannot well co-exist, or flourish together. One must, in time, give way to the other, and the weak must in the end be supplanted by the strong. But it cannot be violently wrenched out of place and cast aside. Nations cannot be made to change their habits and methods and modes of thought in a day. To bring the Indian to look at things from our standpoint is a work requiring time, patience, and the skill as well as the benign spirit of Christian statesmanship. Let us first demonstrate, on a small scale, the practicability of the plans we propose; and when we have done that, if we can do it, a persevering patience will be needed to make the policy general.

(III) The theory that the Indian is a man and a citizen, able to take care of himself, possessed of the attributes of manhood in their broadest sense, and fully responsible to all the laws of our civilized life—a man like other men, and therefore to be treated exactly as other men—is embodied in the first part of this bill, which provides for giving every Indian a farm, and leaving him then to take care of himself, because, as is assumed by the framers of the bill, he *is* able to take care of himself; but having thus launched the Indian upon his future course of life, the bill turns round upon itself and, assuming that the Indian *is not* and *will not* be able to take care of himself, at once proceeds to hedge him around with provisions intended to prevent him from exercising any of the rights of a land-owner except that of working and living on his allotment. He cannot sell, mortgage, lease, or in any way alienate his land; and although he is to be under and amenable to the laws, he is to be free from taxation for all purposes. He is to be treated as a man in giving him land and exacting from him the duty of maintaining himself upon and off of it, and all this upon the plea that he is simply a man, who is to be treated as other men are; and then, as soon as we do this, we proceed to treat him as a child, an infant, a ward in chancery, who is unable to take care of himself and therefore needs the protecting care of government. If he *is* able to take care of himself, all this precaution is unnecessary; if he is *not* able to take care of himself, all this effort to make him try to do it is illogical. If the Indian is a ward under the paternal care of government, he might as well hold his lands in common as in severalty. He cannot be made to feel the pride which a man feels in the ownership of property while he is made to feel that he does not possess one single attribute of separate ownership in the soil. In this respect the bill is like the old constitution of Virginia, which, when the convention which framed it put into it a clause providing a method for amending it, was said by John Randolph to bear upon its face the sardonic grin of death.

The main purpose of this bill is not to help the Indian, or solve the Indian problem, or provide a method for getting out of our Indian troubles so much as it is to provide a method for getting at the valuable Indian lands and opening them up to white settlement. The main object of the bill is in the last sections of it, not in the first. The sting of this animal is in its tail. When the Indian has got his allotments, the rest of the land is to be put up to the highest bidder, and he is to be surrounded in his allotments with a wall of fire, a cordon of white settlements, which will gradually but surely hem him in, circumscribe him, and eventually crowd him out. True, the proceeds of the sale are to be invested for the Indians; but when the Indian is smothered out, as he will be under the operations of this bill, the investment will revert to the national Treasury, and the Indian, in the long run, will be none the better for it, for nothing can be surer than the eventual extermination of the Indian under the operation of this bill.

The real aim of this bill is to get at the Indian lands and open them up to settlement. The provisions for the apparent benefit of the Indian are but the pretext to get at his lands and occupy them. With that accomplished, we have securely paved the way for the extermination of the Indian races upon this part of the continent. If this were done in the name of Greed, it would be bad enough; but to do it in the name of Humanity, and under the cloak of an ardent desire to promote the Indian's welfare by making him like ourselves, whether he will or not, is infinitely worse. Of all the attempts to encroach upon the Indian, this attempt to manufacture him into a white man by act of Congress and the grace of the Secretary of the Interior is the baldest, the boldest, and the most unjustifiable.

Whatever civilization has been reached by the Indian tribes has been attained under the tribal system, and not under the system proposed by this bill. The Cherokees, Choctaws, Chickasaws, Creeks, and Seminoles, all five of them barbarous tribes within the short limit of our own history as a people, have all been brought to a creditable state of advancement under the tribal system. The same may be said of the Sioux and Chippewas, and many smaller tribes. Gradually, under that system they are working out their own deliverance, which will come in their own good time if we but leave them alone and perform our part of the many contracts we have made with them. But that we have never yet done and it seems from this bill we will never yet do. We want their lands and we are bound to have them. Let those take a part in despoiling them who will; for ourselves, we believe the entire policy of this bill to be wrong, ill-timed, and unstatesmanlike; and we put ourselves on record against it as about all that is now left us to do, except to vote against the bill on its final passage.

RUSSELL ERRETT.
CHAS. E. HOOKER.
T. M. GUNTER.

2

Senate Debate on Severalty

The only significant congressional debate on the philosophy of allotment took place in late January 1881, over the severalty legislation (S. 1773) introduced by Senator Richard Coke, Democrat from Texas. The debate was notable primarily for the eloquent skepticism of Senator Henry Teller of Colorado who rejected the arguments of his colleagues in the Senate, of religious leaders in the pulpit, and others who urged the passage of the bill as a boon to the Indian. Teller predicted that if it became law it would be found in its operation "to be a law of destruction instead of a law of benefaction" and opposed its application to the Indian Territory, as urged by Senator Vest.

Document†

Mr. Coke: Mr. President, I hope the amendment of the Senator from Missouri [Mr. Vest] will be voted down. The bill as presented by the committee excludes the Indian Territory from its operations. One reason among others for this exclusion is, the bill provides that after the amount of land is allotted to the individual Indian, the Secretary of the Interior shall contract for the remainder for the Government, and invest the purchase money for the Indians. If the United States Government acquires in the Indian Territory any more land it will be another bone of contention in that Territory in addition to that which the honorable Senator from Missouri says is about producing a war there, because the white men are claiming the right to go upon it and occupy it as public land. Not desiring to complicate the Indian Territory any further than it is already complicated, we therefore excluded it entirely from the operation of the bill. Whatever remedy the Indians of the Indian Territory may desire on this subject can be given them by a separate bill. This is a general bill, applicable to all Indians except those in the Indian Territory. As I remarked to the Senator from Missouri this morning, when he told me of this amendment, if it were presented in a separate bill I would give it a consideration that I cannot give it when offered

---

†From: U.S., Congress, Senate, Debate on Bill to Provide Lands in Severalty, Jan. 20, 1881, from *Congressional Record*, 46th Congress, 3rd Session, as reprinted in Wilcomb E. Washburn, ed., *The American Indian and the United States: A Documentary History*, 4 vols. (New York: Random House, 1973), pp. 1700-1704.

as an amendment to this measure. I could, perhaps, propose an amendment to it that would make it acceptable to me if offered as a separate bill, but I cannot consent, if I can avoid it, that it shall be engrafted upon this bill.

With reference to the remarks of the honorable Senator from Colorado, [Mr. Teller] he seems to complain that in his ideas of Indian policy he is at war with the President, he is at war with the Secretary of the Interior, he is at war with the Commissioner of Indian Affairs, he is at war with the peace commissioners, he is at war with the Committee on Indian Affairs of the Senate, and although he did not say it, I will say that he is at war with his own colleague, the Senator from Colorado, [Mr. Hill,] upon the same questions. He says that he has been thwarted by all these personal and official agencies in the enforcement of his views upon the Indian question. He is like the juror who was thwarted by eleven contumacious jurors. That I regret, I would like for the honorable Senator from Colorado to agree with the Committee on Indian Affairs and with other gentlemen who are specially charged with the administration of Indian affairs. As he unfortunately does not agree with us, all that we have left to us is to do the best we can in the absence of the Senator from concurrence in our counsels.

With reference to this bill, it confides a sound discretion in the President of the United States to order a survey of Indian reservations and an allotment of lands to individual Indians whenever the President believes that the lands are such that the Indians can make a living upon them and the Indians desire to make the effort and to take the land in severalty. When these conditions concur, when the Indians desire the lands allotted and desire to work for their living on land of their own, and the lands are capable of yielding them a support, the President is authorized to have the land surveyed and allotted to them in severalty. That is all there is in the bill. The rest is simply an arrangement of detail, providing how much shall be given to each head of a family and how much shall be given to others not heads of families, providing for the issuance of patents, providing for surveys of the land, all, however, depending upon the two great precedent conditions, that the Indians are willing and that the President believes in his discretion that they ought to be given these lands in severalty and allowed to work for their own living. That is all there is of it.

The bill is asked for by the Secretary of the Interior, it is asked for by the Commissioner of Indian Affairs, it is asked for by the Senate Committee on Indian Affairs, it is asked for by the peace commissioners, and it is asked for by the public sentiment of the country which understands the Indian question.

There was a memorial laid upon my table this morning from a number of gentlemen of great intelligence, who visited the committee in person to urge the passage of this bill, representative men of one of the leading Christian denominations. They urge, as the honorable Senator from Missouri has so eloquently done on more occasions than today, that these Indians be given homes; that they be placed upon their own resources; that the benefits of education be granted them, and that an honest effort be made to place their feet in the path that leads to American citizenship. This bill is a commencement in that direction.

As I remarked a few minutes ago, this bill is not an experiment. Allotments have been successfully made before. As a result of the experience of the Indian Department, it is urging a general law under which, as fast as it may be done, it can put all the Indians in the country on the same road to civilization and prosperity that is now enjoyed by some of the Indians who have received allotments in severalty heretofore.

While I am up, I will take occasion to say that, although I have differed with the Secretary of the Interior in his administration of the Indian Department in some respects, in my judgment that official has produced a most beneficent change in the affairs and in the condition of the Indians. A great change, and a beneficent one, has been made—a change the extent of which is developing daily; and if a liberal policy is pursued, such as may be pursued under the pending bill, will show in the future much greater benefits than have already occurred.

I hope, Mr. President, that the bill will pass. I hope that the amendment offered by the honorable Senator from Missouri will not be adopted, because it will complicate the bill; it will introduce questions into this discussion which I for one do not wish to discuss in the consideration of this measure.

Mr. Teller: It is true, sir, that upon this legislation I have not agreed perhaps with the President. I do not know whether I have agreed with him or not. I have not agreed with the committee, or at least I did not last spring; I have not agreed with the Secretary of the Interior; and I did not agree with my colleague also. I found after that disagreement I was very much in the condition that old Stephenson, of England, the great railway engineer, said the cow would be when it met the train. When he was first putting out the project of an engine for a railroad some one said, "Suppose a cow should get on the track and meet the train." He said it would be disastrous to the cow. It was disastrous to me, I admit, that I did not agree with them; that is, I lost the amendments that I offered here; but that does not discourage me very much. I do not govern myself upon questions of this kind by my success or want of success. I said that that was no fit place to put the Indians. The Secretary said it was a desirable place, the committee said it was desirable, my colleague said it was desirable; and yet I find upon the files of the Senate a bill introduced by my colleague to send these Indians to the Uintah reservation. If I disagreed with my colleague then, I am agreeing with him now and he is agreeing with me. He has got around to my position, and I have no doubt in due time the committee will get to my position and the Secretary will get to my position. All they need to do is to find out the facts, because I admit that they are trying to do what is right. I am not complaining that the commissioners or the Secretary or anybody else is trying to do an improper thing, but I say they are proceeding without a knowledge of the facts.

While I am up I want to say another thing about this bill. You propose to divide all this land and to give each Indian his quarter-section, or whatever he may have, and for twenty-five years he is not to sell it, mortgage it, or dispose of it in any shape, and at the end of that time he may sell it. It is safe to predict that when that shall have been done, in thirty years thereafter there will not be an Indian on the continent, or there will be very few at least, that will have any land. That has been the experience wherever we have given land to Indians and guarded it as well as we might and as well as we could; they have eventually got rid of the land and the land has been of no particular benefit to them. I know it will be said, "Why, in twenty-five years they will be all civilized; these people will be church-going farmers, having schools and all the appliances of civilized life in twenty-five years." Mr. President, the other day I went into the Library and I took up the report of old Jedediah Morse, made in 1818 or 1822—I do not remember which—on Indian affairs when Indian affairs were under the control of the War Department. No man can read that report and not come to the conclusion that ten or fifteen years at the furthest would see a solution of all these difficulties, because in that length of time the Indians were to be civilized. Mr. Morse told what progress they were making; he told about the prayer-meetings that the female Indians were holding, and he told about the religious zeal among the Indians all over the country and what strides they were making in civilization. That has been the cry every year since. You may go back fifteen years ago—and I have done it and examined them—and take the reports of the agents for these very Ute Indians, and you would suppose each year that the next year there would be very little use of an agent and the year after none at all. Every agent who goes out, who is sent out, is desirous of making good reports. He goes to the Indians, and he probably does his best, at least many of the agents do, to civilize them, and if he is a man who does not he is more sure to report to his superior, the Commissioner, that his Indians are making great progress and that in a little while they will all be civilized and enlightened Indians.

Now, divide up this land and you will in a few years deprive the Indians of a resting-place on the face of this continent; and no man who has studied this question intelligently, and who has the Indian interest at heart, can talk about dividing this land and giving them tracts in severalty till they shall have made such progress in civilization that they know the benefits and the advantages of land in severalty, and of a fee-simple absolute title; and the whole Presbyterian Church and all other churches all over this country cannot convince me, with an observation of twenty years, and, I believe, a heart that beats as warmly for the Indians as that of any other man living, that that is in the interest of the Indians. It is in the interest of speculators; it is in the interest of the men who are clutching up this land, but not in the interest of the Indians at all; and there is the baneful feature of it that when you have allotted the Indians land on which they cannot make a living the Secretary of the Interior may then proceed to purchase their land, and Congress will, as a matter of course, ratify the purchase, and the Indians will become the owners in a few years in fee, and away goes their title, and, as I said before, they are wanderers over the face of this continent, without a place whereon to lay their heads. And yet every man who raises his voice against a bill of this kind is charged with not looking to the interest of the Indians, and I am met by the astonishing argument that because the Secretary of the Interior, and because the Committee on Indian Affairs, (for whose opinion I have due and proper respect,) and because public sentiment say that they should have land in severalty, I am running amuck against all the intelligence and all the virtue of the country, and therefore I must be wrong.

Mr. President, what I complain of in connection with this Indian business is that practical common sense is not applied to it. Sentiment does not do the Indians any good. It does not educate them and feed them for us to pass high-sounding resolutions and to put upon the statute-book enactments that declare they shall be protected in their rights.

Furthermore, it does not accomplish the great purposes of civilization to send a few wild Indians down to Hampton and a few up to Carlisle. The Indians cannot be educated by such methods. We must put the schools in the Indian community; we must bring the influences where a whole Indian tribe or a whole band will be affected and influenced by them. It is folly to suppose that this will civilize them.

If I stand alone in the Senate, I want to put upon the record my prophecy in this matter, that when thirty or forty years shall have passed and these Indians shall have parted with their title, they will curse the hand that was raised professedly in their defense to secure this kind of legislation, and if the people who are clamoring for it understood Indian character, and Indian laws, and Indian morals, and Indian religion, they would not be here clamoring for this at all.

3
Senator Dawes Seeks a Solution

Dawes's informal letter to Teller is a remarkable expression of the Massachusetts' senator's true feeling about the inadequacy of the proposed severalty solution to the Indian "problem." Yet he had no plan of his own to suggest and hoped that Teller would supply one. Perhaps he perceived, in Teller's Senate speeches of the previous year, that the Colorado senator, now secretary of the interior, had the knowledge and skill to be able to effect a solution satisfactory to both Indians and whites.

Document†

Pittsfield, Mass.
Sept. 19, 1882

Hon. H. M. Teller
Secy of the Interior

My dear Sir:

I am not doing much campaign work this fall and am therefore tempted to write you a letter about the Indians.

I had the conviction forced upon me by the current of events during the last session more than ever before that a new phase of the Indian question is close upon us for which we are not at all prepared. I wanted to talk it over with you before leaving Washington but had no opportunity. I know that you are in the Interior department not merely for the purpose of living from hand to mouth but rather to accomplish something which will make your administration of it worthy of remembrance and it seems to me that if you will be prepared to meet and cope with the new difficulties which the Indian question is going to force upon you in the near future, you will win plaudits and accomplish lasting good. I see unmistakeable signs that you will have the whole Indian race, "five nations" and all on your hands with no place to put them. I have never seen such an advance made upon them as has been made this last year. "Civilization" has got after these possessions with a greed never

†From: Henry L. Dawes to Henry M. Teller, September 19, 1882, Dawes Papers, Library of Congress, Washington, D.C.

before equalled but it is idle to expect to stay it and worse than folly to shut our eyes to the consequences.

The determination by Congress to put Railroads through the Indian Territory under the power of "Eminent domain" regardless of treaty stipulations puts that whole territory hereafter at the mercy of a majority in Congress; and railroad lines with all that follows after them will be sure to traverse it in every direction as fast as railroads can be built. "Oklahoma" and Capt. Paine and Kansas Emigration will then laugh at those who oppose them.

The United States will sweep its arms around this territory and make it a part of itself. We ran railroads last session in almost every direction through Indian reservations and that being done a reservation as such is as sure to melt away as a snowbank under the sun. We cleared them out of the vast Turtle Mountain region and immigration burst in like a pent up flood and swept over domain enough for a state. We provided for the sale of half the Omaha reservation and began to do the same with the great Sioux reservation. In Arizona and New Mexico we are huddling the Indians together and appropriating to sale and settlement every acre thus relieved of their occupation.

A bill is pending to appoint a commission to reduce the area and run the lines anew of all reservations. An uncontrollable spirit is abroad in the land to appropriate to what is called the "demands of civilization" every foot of desirable land now occupied by the Indians. You cannot resist it: Congress instead of resisting it will help it on. Before you get out of the Interior Department you will have well nigh 200,000 Indians in your hands with no fit Indian lands on which to put them.

What can you do with them? We may cry out against the violation of treaties, denounce flagrant disregard of inalienable rights and the inhumanity of our treatment of the defenseless and all that but the fact remains the same and there will come of this outcry, however just, no practical answer to this question. We are all talking about "land in severalty" for the Indian, treating him as white men are treated by giving him the benefit of and making him obey the laws like any other citizen. All this is well in theory but you and I know that it will not meet the present practical difficulty. Two hundred thousand savages who cannot read a word of any language or speak a word of English, who were never taught to work and don't know how to earn their living nor care to learn, who can't read or be made to comprehend the laws they are expected to obey as citizens or know what is meant by a Court of Justice instituted to enforce them, or even the law of *meum et tuum*, the foundation of society, cannot be set up in severalty and left to stand alone any more than so many reeds, can no more be turned loose on society and bid to confide in and respect an unknown and invisible power relied on to enforce right and punish wrong than so many wild beasts. Without doubt these Indians are to be somehow absorbed into and become a part of the 50,000,000 of our people. There does not seem to be any other way to deal with them. But how? This is what troubles me and this is what I want you to answer in your annual report to Congress. It does not seem to me that the answer can be delayed another session. And you are the only one from position and power and knowledge of Indian character who can do it. There will be all sorts of plans impracticable and visionary introduced into Congress, and we shall drift no one can tell where. The administration and you as its organ should take command of this question and be the first with a well considered measure adequate to the exigency and be prepared to push it. You may depend upon my co-operation in Congress and my readiness to do whatever is necessary there. I do not write this because I have any plan of my own but because I have none and at the same time see a combination of irresistible forces driving the Indians in upon us a great deal faster than we shall be prepared to deal with them. Feeding them in reservations is bad enough. You cannot wait for the children to be educated at Carlisle & Hampton for you are going to have the adults on your hands with no land in reservation worth anything to put them on. All ordinary processes of absorption are slow and scarcely perceptible in their effect upon the whole. They will prove as impotent to solve the problem as colonization was to exterminate slavery. Nor can absorption, any more than amalgamation be forced. The whole subject is surrounded with difficulties but if I can only induce you to take hold of it in earnest I am sure of a practical solution. There is no escape from it and it is the part of wisdom to be found prepared for it when it comes. I hope to be in Washington the first of next month and shall be glad to talk the matter over with you if you should desire it.

            I am truly yours,
            H. L. Dawes

4
The Support of the Indian Rights Association for Land in Severalty Bill

The following description of the bill introduced by Senator Richard Coke of Texas was prepared by Henry S. Pancoast, chairman of the committee on laws of the Indian Rights Association, and published by the association in 1884. The Indian Rights Association continued to support general severalty legislation, even when more coercive provisions were added (*Alternatives 3 and 4*).

Document†

Land in Severalty for Indians, *As Provided for by the Coke Bill.*

For many years past those who have given earnest thought to the best method of placing the Indian on a right footing among us, and patient effort to accomplish this result, have united in the belief that the allotment of land to individual Indians by a secure title would prove one of the most powerful agencies in the advancement of the race.

It has been often pointed out that we have by our policy taken from the Indian the ordinary and essential stimulus to labor. While under our system of pauperizing Indians by the issuing of rations we deprive them of the ordinary necessity for self support, by our refusal to protect them in the possession of their land and by our incessant removals we take away the common motives for cultivating it. The great mass of men work from the imperative necessity

---

†From: Henry S. Pancoast, *Indian Land in Severalty As Provided For By The Coke Bill*, Forty-eighth Congress, First Session, S. 48 (Philadelphia, 1884), pp. 3-7.

for self-support, and from the knowledge that the law will protect them in the possession of their rightful earnings. We have so alienated the Indian from all natural and general conditions, we have placed him in such an artificial and unjust position, that he has neither the necessity for self-support nor any proper protection in the result of his labor. It is a matter of surprise to all who fairly consider all the elements in the case, not that the result is no better, but that it is not far worse.

To give the Indian, then, a secure title to land, so that he may have the assurance of reaping what he has sown, is the plainest justice and good policy.

The thought and labor of those who have long worked for this end has taken shape in a most carefully and skillfully prepared bill for the allotment to Indians in severalty of land on the reservations. This bill is the outcome of long and intimate experience in the condition of the various Indian tribes; the result of a rare combination of practical knowledge and legal training. Its passage will greatly affect for the better the lives of nearly three hundred thousand human beings, besides the incalculable and yet wider influence in the life of a race and in the settlement of a question of national importance. The bill passed the Senate at the last session of the present Congress, and only its passage by the House of Representatives this coming winter is required to make it a law.

§ I. *By the first section* the President is authorized to issue patents for Indian reservations, set apart by treaty or act of Congress, in favor of the several tribes occupying them. Under these patents the United States is to hold the patented land in trust for the several tribes for twenty-five years, and at the end of that time to convey it by patent to the different tribes clear of encumbrance. The President is also given authority to delay in any case the issuing of the final patent if he considers it best for the Indians to do so. These patents are to be recorded and open to inspection.

This first section simply secures the tribe *as such* in the possession of its reservation. It places the strong restraint of the law upon the unjust occupation of Indian lands in the incessant push of Western settlement.

§ II. *The second section* authorizes the President, whenever he thinks it for the best interests of the Indians on a reservation, to have it surveyed or resurveyed, and to allot it to the Indians in severalty—to the heads of families one-quarter, to single persons over eighteen one-eighth, and to orphan children under eighteen one-eighth of a section; to other persons under eighteen one-sixteenth of a section. If there is not sufficient land on a reservation to make such allotment, the land is to be allotted pro rata.

Treaty stipulations setting apart a reservation and providing for the allotment of land in larger quantities are to be fulfilled. The taking of land for grazing purposes by two or more Indians in common is provided for.

§ III. *In section third* provision is made for the manner in which the allotments are to be selected by the Indians, with the proviso that if such selection is not made within five years from the direction to take allotments the agent shall

§ IV. be directed to select for Indians failing to do so. The allotments are to be made under such rules as the Secretary of the Interior may prescribe by agents specially appointed by the President.

§ V. Any Indian not residing upon a reservation or belonging to a tribe for which no reservation has been provided is entitled to settle upon unappropriated land of the United States, and on applying to the local land office can have the land allotted to him and to his children in the same manner as Indians residing on a reservation take allotments under the act. The fees of the local land office are to be paid out of the United States Treasury.

§ VI. *The sixth section* provides that patents shall be issued to individual allottees, declaring that the United States will hold the land in trust for the allottee or his heirs for twenty-five years, and then convey it to him or them absolutely and clear of all encumbrance. The land cannot be conveyed or charged during the time it is so held in trust, and the patents to individual allottees shall override the patent issued to the tribe. After the issue of patents the land shall descend according to the law of the State or Territory in which a reservation is situated. After all the lands on a reservation have been allotted, *or sooner, if the President deem it for the best interests of the Indians*, the Secretary of the Interior may negotiate with a tribe for the purchase of any unallotted portion of its reservation. This purchase is not complete until ratified by Congress. The principal of the purchase-money shall be held by the United States for twenty-five years to the credit of the tribe, and the interest at five percent, paid annually to the Secretary of the Interior, to be applied to the education and support of the tribe. After twenty-five years, by express authority of Congress, the principal shall be payable to the tribe. Proper provision is made for religious bodies now occupying land on the reservations.

§ VII. *Section Seventh* extends over a tribe, upon the completion of the allotments, the laws, both civil and criminal, of the State or Territory in which they reside, and prohibits the passage by the local government of any law denying Indians the equal protection of the law.

VIII. *Section Eighth*, in view of the important fact that the value of land in the West often depends largely upon its proper irrigation, authorizes the Secretary of the Interior to prescribe such rules as he may deem necessary to secure a just distribution of water among the Indians.

§ IX. *Section Ninth* excepts the five civilized tribes of Indian Territory and the Seneca Indians of New York from the provisions of the act.

§ X. *Section Tenth* appropriates one hundred thousand dollars for the survey or resurvey of reservations necessary under the act, and provides that the sum expended be repaid out of the proceeds from the sale of reservation lands.

§ XI. *Section Eleventh* provides that, except as to the issuing of the tribal patents, the provisions of the act shall not extend to any tribe *as such* until the consent of two-thirds adult male members shall have been obtained, but that, notwithstanding this, the President may make allotments to *individual Indians* in the manner provided irrespective of the consent of the two-thirds.

XII. *Section Twelfth* provides that the act shall not affect the right of Congress to grant a right of way for railroads, highways, or telegraph lines for the public use through any lands granted to an Indian or to a tribe upon just compensation being made.

The provisions of this act have been thus stated somewhat in detail because an exact understanding of it is considered most desirable, and because only a close examination reveals the wisdom and care with which many contingencies and possible difficulties have been provided for.

The Main Points of the Bill. The broad and general advantages of the bill may be summed up in a few words. It secures the tribes in possession of their reservations, and ends the notorious wrong of taking the Indian's land by fraud or force without his consent. The United States is to hold the reservations in trust for the tribes, but not as a permanent arrangement. The bill contemplates the breaking up of the entire reservation system; it contemplates the protection of Indian land from the grasp of unscrupulous whites only until the Indian has been given the proper training and preparation to enable him to take care of his own. In the meanwhile, the bill provides an important part of this training. On the consent of two-thirds of the adult males, allotments are to be made to a whole tribe in severalty. The reservations are divided into separate farms, the members of the tribe are given time to firmly plant and settle themselves before, by the extinguishment of the trust in which the reservation is held for the tribe, they are left to take care of themselves. Should the consent of the two-thirds not be obtained, the individual Indians can at once take allotments under the act. There is neither a compulsion of the majority nor the slightest disregard of the wants of the minority. The law of the white man is to be extended when, by the completion of the allotments, the Indians have shown themselves reasonably fit for it. Nor does the act overlook the undoubted fact that it is neither wise nor right to let these great, solid blocks of reservations stand in the way of traffic and settlement. Right of way through Indian land can be granted at any time to railroads, highways, and telegraph companies, and, at *any time* unallotted land can be purchased, proper compensation being given. Such is the wise admixture in this bill of what is best in the views of those who regard this question from a radical or a conservative standpoint; land in severalty is to be given at once to all who desire it; the Indian is protected against the greed of the whites; a process of tribal disintegration is at once started, and the blotting out of the reservations as fast as it can be safely done, is the ultimate object of the bill.

In the light of the lasting importance of this measure to so many who are unrepresented among the legislators we have selected to do our will, you are asked to fairly and honestly consider it, and if it seems to you desirable and right, you are most earnestly and respectfully reminded that there rests on you a personal responsibility to give your influence, your time and thought, to secure its passage.

Henry S. Pancoast,

October 9th, 1884.

Chairman of the Committee on Laws.

5
The Beginnings of Compulsory Allotment

The genesis of the coercive policy of forced allotment and the practical measures by which it was to be brought about, emerged from the meeting called by Dr. Lyman Abbott, editor of *The Christian Union* of New York, and held in its offices on July 7, 1885, prior to the annual conference of humanitarians at Lake Mohonk in October. Although the least knowledgeable in Indian affairs of all those gathered there, Dr. Abbott was able to put the impress of his beliefs and his method upon the Indian reform movement (*Alternative 4*).

Document†

Proceedings of Informal Indian Meeting Held by Request
of Dr. Lyman Abbott

On Tuesday July 7th at 11 A.M. an informal meeting was held at the office of the Christian Union, Lafayette Place, New York, for a consideration of the Indian Question. This meeting was called at the suggestion and by the invitation of Dr. Lyman Abbott, and was intended to accomplish a general preparation of the work subsequently to be undertaken by the Mohonk Conference and to facilitate the operations of that body. Those present at this meeting were Dr. Lyman Abbott, Editor of the Christian Union, Gen. E. Whittlesey, Secretary of the Board of Indian Commissioners, Gen. S. C. Armstrong, of Hampton, Virginia, Miss Alice G. Fletcher, of the Cambridge Museum of Technology, Dr. James E. Rhoads, Vice President Indian Rights Association, Capt. R. H. Pratt, Supt. of the Carlisle Indian Training School, Albert K. Smiley Esq., of the Board of Indian Commissioners, and Herbert Welsh, Cor. Secretary of the Indian Rights Association. Dr. James E. Rhoads was chosen as Chairman of the meeting, and Herbert Welsh as Secretary. The work of the meeting was begun by Dr. Abbott reading to those present a

---

†From: "Lyman Abbot's Meeting," Dawes Papers, General Correspondence, Box 27, Library of Congress.

paper prepared by Gen. Armstrong in which a proposed Indian policy was outlined. The main points of this policy, as presented in Gen. Armstrong's paper were 1st Education, 2nd Land. 3rd Law. A copy of this paper had been sent, previous to the meeting in the office of the Christian Union, to all those who were to be present at the meeting, with the request that they would suggest such alterations in it as might seem to them desirable. The only changes suggested were offered by Miss Fletcher, who desired a more definite statement than had been given by Gen. Armstrong, as to how the three points aimed at were to be reached; by Capt. Pratt who desired education to be considered as the most important factor in the civilization of the Indian; by Herbert Welsh who suggested that the proposed opening of Indian lands to white settlement should be done without violation of existing treaties or after such treaties had been modified with the consent of the Indians. Dr. Abbott then made a brief statement of a plan by which the Indian policy, submitted by Gen. Armstrong, might be carried into execution. This plan was purposely framed in a manner likely to promote discussion; it was not contended in behalf of it that it was complete, but simply that it would open the subject and lead to something more perfect. Dr. Abbott stated that the time had come when the best men of the west and of the east must be in harmony in order to bring about the solution of the Indian question, and action in the matter to be effective must be prompt. This plan, as suggested by Dr. Abbott, and as modified and agreed to after discussion by the members of the meeting, was as follows:

A new Commission shall be appointed by the President, the members of which shall be salaried and to which the Secretary of the Interior and the Indian Commissioner shall belong. The tenure of office of this Commission shall be five years. Its object shall be to carry out under existing treaties, as far as possible, the following ends. In cases after every honorable and just effort has been used in vain to induce Indians to conform with the humane purposes of the Nation, treaties are found to impede the work to be accomplished the Commission may take steps to procure their modification or abrogation.

SECOND. The Commission shall be empowered to appoint Agents to carry out its work.

THIRD. The Commission shall allot lands to the Indians in such amounts and under such terms as are in general indicated by the provisions of the Coke Bill. The Commission shall allow the Indians 3 (?) years in which to select lands, and if at the end of that time any Indian shall not have done so the Commission shall select lands for them. At the end of   years all Indians shall be placed in the individual possession of lands and all issue of rations shall cease. The Coke bill shall be modified to include these provisions.

The Commission shall devise a comprehensive system of education, which shall place all Indian Children in Industrial schools and which shall bring all adult Indians under the experiences of civilized life. All adult Indians shall also be brought so far as possible under preparation for self-support by work. The funds for these purposes shall be derived as largely as possible from the proceeds of the sale of lands.

A sufficient number of farmers and other industrial teachers shall be provided to train the adult Indians in civilized pursuits.

When the Commission shall have allotted to each Indian such amount of land as shall seem to them to be sufficient, the surplus lands shall be appraised at their just and equitable value and shall be purchased by the United States and the proceeds applied to the education and benefit of the Indians. All patents for Indian lands shall be made out by local land offices. All removal of Indian tribes must cease.

6

Pressures for "Prompt" and Compulsory Allotment

Abbott was careful to apprise Senator Dawes of the results of the meeting described in Document 5, and continued to present his view to the influential senator in as persuasive a fashion as possible. In the following letter, which anticipated the crucial Lake Mohonk meeting, Abbott insisted on the importance of compulsory and prompt allotment of lands, thus helping to set the stage for the torpedoing of the milder Coke bill (*Alternative 4*).

Document†

Cornwall-on-Hudson, N.Y.,
July 20, 1885.

My Dear Mr. Dawes:

Thank you for your note of July 15th, which I wish I might have printed in the Christian Union. As it was personal to me I had no right to do that; but I have adopted and used a part of it, without referring to you, in an editorial paragraph.

I am not unfamiliar with the Coke Bill, and joined cordially with others at Lake Mohonk in urging its adoption by Congress, and if other arrangements would have permitted should have gone on last Winter to Washington with a delegation for that purpose. We have urged it also through the Christian Union. I would not venture to offer amendments in detail; but there are three amendments in principle which seem to me desirable.

1. Section First provides for issuing patents to Indian tribes for their reservations. I think this will increase the difficulty of breaking up the reservations, and I would do nothing in that direction.

2. Section Second authorizes the President to take measures for the allotment of land in severalty. I would require not authorize the allotment of land; and on the same principle, instead of negotiating (Section 6) for the

---

†From: Lyman Abbott to Henry L. Dawes, July 20, 1885, Dawes Papers, General Correspondence, Box 27, Library of Congress.

purchase of unallotted lands I would, unless such negotiations could be carried through promptly and successfully, appraise the land and take it at the appraised valuation, on the same principle that we take land for a railroad or a public park, the proceeds to be invested for the benefit of Indian schools and civilizing agencies.

3. To accomplish these results I would create a Commission, appointed by the President with the advice of the Senate, if possible non-partisan, at all events with tenure sufficiently permanent to enable it to last as long as the work lasted, to carry out the policy of allotment in connection with the Interior Department. Under our Constitution the personnel of the Administration is likely to change every four years, and four years is not time enough in which to carry any policy through to its consummation.

I am in hearty sympathy with the general purposes of the Coke Bill, but I should like to see the allotment compulsory instead of voluntary, prompt instead of gradual, and under a permanent commission instead of under a shifting administration. It seems to me that we have tried pretty thoroughly the experiment of civilizing and educating the Indians on a reservation before distributing them among the people, and we failed for two reasons; first, because the Indian on the reservation lacks all the civilizing agencies which are incidental to a civilized community; and second, because we cannot guard against corruption, or incompetence, or both, in the Government itself; and the consequence is that honest and law-abiding citizens are kept out of the reservation, while scamps and rascals and cow-boys get in. I would, therefore, abandon this experiment, abolish the reservation, allow only time enough to work out the abolition, scatter the Indians among the white people, make their lands inalienable for a term of years, give them the rights of citizenship, and trust for their protection to the general laws of the land. It seems to me a little absurd to be writing this to you who have made such a study of Indian affairs, while I know so little about them; but I am warmly interested in the Indian problem, and if it is the good fortune of the editor that he can always speak on every subject to an audience generally prepossessed in his favor, it is his misfortune that he is often required to speak on topics without adequate previous knowledge. I shall be very glad if you can at any time dictate to your amanuensis any information which I can use to advantage in our columns, editorial or otherwise, in promoting the general cause of justice and humanity which we both have so much to heart.

I thank you very heartily for your kind invitation to visit and confer with you at Pittsfield. I am afraid that is impossible at present; but I hope we may meet at Lake Mohonk in October.

Yours Sincerely,

Lyman Abbott

7

A Protest Against Forced Allotment

The *Council Fire* was always out of step with the general run of Indian reformers, and its reaction to the Lake Mohonk resolution of 1885 was typical of its skeptical approach (*Alternative 3*). It called particular attention to the elevated rhetoric in which the coercive recommendations of the reformers at Lake Mohonk were clothed. Although presenting effective arguments, the *Council Fire* was unable to win sufficient supporters to stop the steamroller that Lyman Abbott and his cohorts had devised.

Document†

The Mohonk Platform

We print below the resolutions adopted at the recent conference on Indian affairs, at Lake Mohonk. The first six lines, constituting the preamble, will meet the hearty approval of all friends of the Indians. Apply the "principles of justice and equal rights" to the Indian question, sacredly guard their property rights and fulfill faithfully all obligations, and the vexed question will be settled for all time.

We believe in the enlargement of the system of education, the preparation for self-support of adult Indians, and the introduction of industrial methods among the various tribes. We approve these planks of the Mohonk platform, but we cannot approve of the proposed means to be employed to give them efficacy. The resolutions, or rather the declaration of principles announced, are singularly inconsistent. The declaration that the principles of justice and equal rights should be applied to the settlement of the Indian question, and that all property rights should be guarded, and all obligations towards the Indians faithfully fulfilled, is not consistent with the declared purpose of breaking up the Indian reservations, and the disposal of certain portions in severalty, whether the Indians are prepared for it or not. Through solemn treaties, the Government has recognized the Indian title to lands, and agreed

†From: *The Council Fire* 8, no. 11 (November 1885): 157-58.

to protect it. Tribal relations have been recognized, and with them the system of holding lands in common. To ignore this title, and disturb the tribal relations, and break up the system of holding land, and destroying the reservations, all supposed to be protected by the solemn covenants entered into between the Indian tribes and the United States Government, would be an act of bad faith, justified on no other ground but that "might makes right."

We are not willing to believe that the professed friends of the Indian who met at Lake Mohonk, had any desire to take from the Indians the lands which belong to them, but the effects of their declaration of principles, touching the treatment of reservations and the division of lands, will add fuel to the flame which unscrupulous men have been feeding for years, that is, the ultimate dispossession of the Indian of the lands which he occupies. Is it not time to call a halt on this spirit of encroachment? Surely if civilization is to practice justice and administer equal rights, the lands of the Indian must be held as sacred as the lands of the white man, and until the desire to sell comes from the Indians, this policy of pressure to force them to give up their reservations should cease. What the Indian stands in need of to-day is the faithful fulfillment of the obligations of the Government toward him. These obligations comprehend the protection of his lands, the introduction of industrial methods, the establishment of schools and the exercise of genuine friendship in assisting him toward a higher plane of civilization. Any policy that seeks honestly the carrying out of these obligations, is a good one and will receive our earnest support; but we shall continue to protest in the future, as we have in the past, against those methods of treatment which require the despoilments of the Indian as an essential step toward his civilization. The platform as adopted reads as follows:

"The Indian question can never be settled except on principles of justice and equal rights. In its settlement all property rights of the Indians should be sacredly guarded and all obligations should be faithfully fulfilled. Keeping this steadily in view the object of all legislative and executive action hereafter, should be, not the isolation of the Indians, but the abrogation of the Indian reservation as rapidly as possible, the permitted diffusion of the Indians among the people, in order that they may become acquainted with the civilized habits and modes of life, the ultimate discontinuance of annuities so promotive of idleness and pauperism, the subjection of the Indians to the laws of the United States and of the States and Territories where they may reside, and their protection by the same laws as those by which citizens are protected, the opening of all the territory of the United States to their possible acquisition, and to civilization and the early admission of Indians to American citizenship. These objects should be steadily kept in view and pursued immediately, vigorously and continuously. The measures we recommend for their accomplishment are the following:

First. The present system of Indian education should be enlarged, and a comprehensive method should be adopted, which shall place all Indian children in schools under compulsion, if necessary, and shall provide industrial education for a large proportion of them. Adult Indians should be brought under preparation for self-support. To this end the free ration system should be discontinued as rapidly as possible, and a sufficient number of farmers and other industrial teachers should be provided, meantime, to teach them to earn their own living.

Second. Immediate measures should be taken to break up the system of holding all lands in common, and each Indian family should receive a patent for a portion of land to be held in severalty, its amount dependent upon the number of members of the family, and the character of the land, whether adapted for cultivation or for grazing. This land should be inalienable for a period of twenty-five years. The Coke bill, as embodying this principle, has our earnest support, and is urged upon all friends of the Indians as the one practicable measure for achieving these ends.

Third. All portions of the Indian reservations which are not so allotted should, after the Indians shall have selected and secured their lands, be purchased by the Government, at a fair rate, and thrown open to settlement.

Fourth. The cash value of the land thus purchased should be set aside by the Government as a fund to be expended as rapidly as can be wisely done for the benefit, especially, of their industrial and educational advancement.

Fifth. In order to carry out the preceding recommendations, equal provisions should be made for the necessary surveys of reservations, and wherever necessary, negotiations should be entered into for the modification of the present treaties, and these negotiations should be pushed, in every honorable way, until the consent of the Indians be obtained.

Sixth. Indians belonging to tribes which give up their reservations and accept allotments of lands in severalty, and all Indians that abandon their tribal organization and adopt the habits and modes of civilized life, should be at once admitted to citizenship of the United States, become subject to and entitled to the protection of the laws of the United States, and of the States or Territories where they may reside.

Seventh. During this process of civilization some representative of the United States Government should be charged with the protection and instruction of the Indians. But all such officers should be withdrawn as soon as the Indians are capable of self-support and self-protection.

Eighth. We are unalterably opposed to the removal of tribes of Indians from their established homes and massing them together in one or more Territories, as injurious to the Indians and an impediment to their civilization.

We thankfully recognize the growing interest taken by the legislative and executive departments of our country in the welfare of the Indian, and the increased desire manifest among our people, West and East, to do them justice; and our thanks are also due to the religious and philanthropic organizations which have fostered their interest and have supplemented the work of the Government by their missionary and educational labors. But we believe that what has been done in the past is but a beginning, and that both government and individuals must do much more before the debt we own the Indians can be paid.

8

"Shall We Persist in A Policy That has Failed?"

The statement of George W. Manypenny, former commissioner of Indian affairs, received less attention than it deserved. Manypenny had negotiated many treaties which provided for allotment of land in severalty. In questioning the appropriateness of the legislation recommended by the Lake Mohonk Conference at its 1885 meeting, he acknowledged his own disillusionment with the treaties he had earlier negotiated. "Had I known then, as I now know, what would result from those treaties," he concluded, "I would be compelled to admit that I had committed a high crime" (*Alternative 2*).

Document†

Shall We Persist In A Policy That Has Failed?
By Hon. G. W. Manypenny

To the Editors of the Council Fire:

The matters presented by Dr. Rhodes, president of the business committee of the Friends of the Indians, at the Mohonk Conference, held early in this month, for the consideration of the Conference, when compared with the views of the minority of the committee on Indian Affairs of the House of Representatives (Messrs. Errett, Hooker and Gunter), in their report against the provisions of the bill introduced by Mr. Scales, the chairman of the Indian committee, on the 28th of April, 1880, discloses the fact that there is diversity of opinion as to the proper mode of solving the "Indian problem" among those who profess to be the true friends of the Indian.

I need not refer here to the views embodied in the minority report of the Indian committee of the House, since your readers have that report in the October number of your paper.

---

†From: George W. Manypenny, "Shall We Persist in a Policy That Has Failed?" *The Council Fire* 8, no. 11 (November 1885): 153-56.

The newspapers gave a report of Dr. Rhodes' introductory speech as the organ of the business committee of the Conference. That gentleman sets out with the declaration that the Indian question can never be settled except upon the principle of justice and equal rights. Keeping this in view, he suggests that among the primary objects for legislation and executive action in the future, are the abrogation of the reservation system, the dissolution of the tribal relation, the subjection of the Indian as a citizen to the law, and his protection as a citizen by the law; the intermingling of the Indians as American citizens with the white race, and the opening of all the territory of the United States, without exception or reservation, to civilization. These objects, it is declared, must be pursued immediately, vigorously and continuously. And to this end he suggests immediate negotiations with all the Indian tribes for their consent to modify or set aside whatever treaties constitute an obstacle to such a policy; and in the event of failure to obtain the consent of the Indians to this policy, after reasonable time and effort, then its execution without their consent. After discussion the propositions submitted were recommitted to the committee, which was increased in numbers. I have not seen the report of the final action of the conference; but am told that the provisions of the Coke bill for the allotment of lands in severalty and also the provisions of the Sioux bill were approved.

I do not care to discuss these matters now, although it is with difficulty that I restrain myself from commenting on some of the utterances of Dr. Rhodes. Sufficient to say that the end he desires to reach by immediate, vigorous and continuous action, will, I have no doubt, meet the hearty approval of the various combinations, whether they be railroad monopolists, land-grabbers, cattle kings or cowboys, who all have their covetous eyes set upon the lands to which the Indian title has not been extinguished.

My purpose at present is to call attention to some transactions in the past, and submit some facts for the consideration of such of our fellow-citizens as take an interest in Indian affairs, and who desire that the red man shall be protected from all experiments that may in the end have an injurious and evil tendency, if they do not, if persisted in, work his ruin and destruction.

Coincident with the adoption of the Constitution, the Ordinance of 1787 was promulgated. It contained these words: "The utmost good faith shall be observed toward the Indians; their lands and property shall never be taken from them without their consent, and in their property, rights and liberty, they shall never be invaded or disturbed, unless in just and lawful wars authorized by Congress." Had there been a faithful observance of the covenants contained in this ordinance, from its adoption to the present period, the condition of our Indian population would be very different from what it now is.

Nearly forty years after the adoption of this ordinance, President Monroe, then approaching the end of his second term, felt called upon to submit a special message to Congress on the Indian question. After referring to the unsatisfactory condition of affairs and the danger to which the Indians were exposed, he said it had been demonstrated that "without a timely anticipation of and provision against the dangers to which they are exposed, under causes which it will be difficult if not impossible to control, their degradation and extermination will be inevitable." As a remedy the President recommended their removal to the country west of the Mississippi, on conditions satisfactory to themselves and honorable to the United States. "This (said he) can be done only by conveying to each tribe a good title to an adequate portion of land to which it may consent to remove, and providing for it there a system of internal government which shall protect their property from invasion, and by regular progress of improvement and civilization prevent that degeneracy which has generally marked the transition from one to the other state." No definite action was taken by Congress until in 1830, President Jackson in his first annual message, dated December 8, 1829, dealt fully with the subject, and recommended the removal of the Indian tribes within the States as a remedy for our Indian troubles and complications. He said; "As a means of effecting this end, I suggest for your consideration the propriety of setting apart an ample district west of the Mississippi, and without the limits of any State or Territory now formed, to be guaranteed to the Indian tribes as long as they shall occupy it, each tribe having the distinct control over the portion designated for its own use. There they may be secured in governments of their own choice, subject to no other control from the United States than such as may be necessary to preserve peace on the frontier and between the several tribes. There the benevolent may endeavor to teach them the arts of civilization, and by promoting union and harmony among them to raise up an interesting commonwealth, destined to perpetuate the race and to attest the humanity of the Government."

On the 28th of May, 1830, the act "To provide for an exchange of lands with the Indians residing within any of the States or Territories, and for their removal west of the river Mississippi" was passed, and under and by authority of that act the country west of Arkansas and Missouri, was designated and dedicated as the permanent homes of the Indians removed to and placed upon it. In the act the President was authorized to "*solemnly* assure the tribes with whom exchanges of lands were made, that the United States would *forever* secure and guarantee to them and their heirs and successors, the country so exchanged with them, and if they prefer it, the United States would cause a patent or grant to be made and executed to them for the same."

It required several years to effect the exchanges with and complete the transfer of such tribes as were persuaded to remove to the lands west of the States of Missouri and Arkansas designated for their permanent homes. Finally the Cherokees, Creeks, Choctaws, Chickasaws and Seminoles were removed to the reservations on which they now dwell, and the Delawares, Shawnees, Miamis, Kickapoos, with different other tribes, were removed to and placed upon lands west of Missouri, now the eastern part of the State of Kansas. In the treaties with the Indians, and by which provision was made for their removal, they were given the most solemn assurances that the lands conveyed to them should be their permanent homes forever, and that in no future time should their reservations be embraced within the limits of any State or Territory or subject to the laws thereof. There they were to dwell secured in governments of their own choice, with no other control from the United States than such as was necessary to preserve peace on the frontier and between the several tribes. The only lawful occupants of this Indian country (other than the Indians) were a few Indian agents and traders, and missionaries representing various religious denominations, with one military post at Fort Leavenworth and one at Fort Gibson, to expel intruders and suppress disorder.

In 1849 emigration from the States to the Pacific slope commenced. Many that journeyed thither by land passed through the Indian reservations west of Missouri, and thus public attention was attracted to the lands occupied by the Indians. It was soon suggested that the Indian title should be extinguished and the country opened for the use and occupation of white men. The land was described as most desirable, and it was affirmed that it was an outrage that it should be in the possession of hordes of savages. The pressure for opening the country became so strong that in 1852 a bill passed the House of Representatives organizing the territory of Nebraska, embracing within its boundaries the Indian reservations west of Missouri. This bill failed in the Senate. A like bill passed the House in 1853, but failed in the Senate. In lieu of this measure, both branches of Congress concurred in an amendment to one of the appropriation bills, by which $50,000 was appropriated to enable the President to cause treaties to be made with the tribes located west of Missouri for the extinguishment of the title to their lands in whole or in part, to the end that a territorial government could be organized.

In July 1853 the President designated me as Commissioner to negotiate with these Indians. In August I visited the Indian country and was with the different tribes at their homes on their reservations that had been assured to them when removed from the States, that they should be permanent and forever. I was with them until near the middle of October. They all received me with courtesy, even kindness, but expressed astonishment when I disclosed the object of my visit and the desire of the government. I found among the various tribes many who had adopted civilized pursuits, and who were laboring diligently to reclaim and lead their brethren forward. There were farmers who dwelt in good houses, with the comforts and conveniences usual among civilized people, others who had rude dwellings and fields under cultivation, and others who still adhered to and dwelt in the tepee.

A number of manual labor schools, under the patronage of the Presbyterian, Catholic, Baptist, and Methodist churches, and the Society of Friends, were established among the Indians. These were supplied with pupils, male and female, by the different tribes, and were doing a good work. Some were crowded with scholars.

As a whole they were peaceable and happy communities. In the removal of each tribe from the States to this promised land, the members suffered on the journey great hardships. Many died on the way, and it required years to overcome the injury sustained by these removals, and to outlive the recollection of the afflictions and trials incident thereto. They had at the time of my visit reached this point, and were in a condition that was hopeful. I made no treaties with them on this visit, but began that work early in 1854, and by midsummer had concluded treaties with the Kickapoo, Sac and Fox, of Missouri, Iowa, Delaware, Miami, Shawnee, Kaskaskia, Peoria, Wea and Piankishaw Indians, and the Territories of Kansas and Nebraska were organized.

The lands within the several reservations, except the quantity necessary for homesteads, was conveyed to the United States, in some cases for specific sums of money, in other cases the conveyance was made in trust, the land to be surveyed and sold as the public lands were, the net proceeds to be paid to the Indians. Provision in each treaty was made for surveying into legal subdivisions the tracts reserved for Indian homesteads, and for the assignment in severalty to the heads of families and all other persons, the equitable portions of such lands to be held in their individual right, with provision that in the future patents should issue to them, with such guards and restrictions as were deemed necessary at the time of issue.

The Wyandotte Indians were an exception. These Indians in 1842 ceded their small reservation in Ohio to the United States, the latter agreeing to furnish them a home west of Missouri. This was not done at once, and the Wyandottes themselves purchased from the Delawares a few townships of land in the Forks of the Kansas and Missouri rivers, and Congress ratified this purchase. Here they dwelt at the time of my visit in 1853. I was astonished at the extent of their improvements. Their land was of good quality, and was being rapidly brought into cultivation. On the north bank of Kansas river, a few miles above its mouth, they had a handsome village called Wyandotte City. Here was their council house, two churches, school house, several stores and a number of private dwellings. Every thing was orderly and business-like about this Indian town, and I was much impressed with what I saw. In the month of January, 1855, a delegation of Wyandottes, duly authorized, visited Washington to make a treaty with the United States. By the 31st of the month a conclusion was reached, and a treaty signed by those delegates and myself.

The Indians ceded to the United States all their right and title to the tract of land in the forks of the Kansas and Missouri rivers, and which they held in common; the object of the cession being that the Government should have the land surveyed and divided into specific tracts, and then reconveyed to the individual members of the Wyandotte Nation by patent in fee simple. This done, the Indians were clothed with full citizenship. These words are quoted from the treaty: "The Wyandotte Indians, having become sufficiently advanced in civilization, and being desirous of becoming citizens, it is hereby agreed and stipulated that their organization and their relations with the United States as an Indian tribe shall be dissolved and terminated on the ratification of this agreement, except so far as the further and temporary continuance of the same may be necessary in the execution of some of the stipulations herein; and from and after the date of such ratification the

Wyandotte Indians, and each and every one of them, except as hereinafter provided, shall be deemed and are hereby declared to be, citizens of the United States to all intents and purposes, and shall be entitled to all the rights, privileges and immunities of such citizens; and shall in all respects be subject to the laws of the United States and the Territory of Kansas, in the same manner as other citizens of said Territory." As soon as appropriations were made for that purpose the work of surveying the lands reserved for the homes of the Indians of the several tribes with whom treaties were made was commenced, to the end that they could be divided into homesteads and assigned in severalty.

Emigrants began to flow into Kansas as soon as the bill organizing the territories passed; and very soon thereafter the homes of the Indians were invaded. The guards and restrictions (of a temporary character) in relation to settlements on the ceded lands were disregarded. Every effort was made by the Indian Office to protect the Indians from the wrong-doing of the white men, but without success. I cannot attempt, in this paper, to go into detail, since it would make it burdensome. I may, however, remark that the determination and unabated desire of the people of Kansas to bereave the Indians of their lands was not satisfied until this object was accomplished; and, by authority of an act of Congress passed in 1863, the Delaware, Shawnee, Miami, Wyandotte, Iowa, Chippewa, Wea and Piankishaw and Kaskaskia and Peoria, and other tribes, to whom the country in Kansas was given as a permanent home, were transferred to the Indian Territory, where they now dwell in their tribal relation.

The treaties which I made and which I thought at the time contained provisions that were wise and judicious, and under which I believed the Indians would rapidly advance, proved to be instruments to disinherit them and despoil them of their noble lands in Kansas.

Now look at the five civilized tribes in the Indian Territory. There they have dwelt on the lands assigned them for half a century in their tribal relation and holding the lands in common, that is, the title is in the tribe. The gross population of these five tribes is about 65,000 souls. The Indian Office report for 1884 gives the aggregate quantity of cereals raised the previous harvest thus: Wheat, 280,000 bushels; corn, 1,615,000 bushels; oats and barley, 313,000 bushels; vegetables, 597,597 bushels. Their cotton crop is generally about 6,000,000 pounds, but as to this crop, as well as the product of hay, etc., there is no report for the year referred to. The aggregate stock owned by these five tribes in 1884 was: Horses, 87,000; mules, 26,570; cattle, 710,000; sheep, 530,000; and swine, 81,000. The Government holds a large amount of funds in trust for them.

They have dispersed among them 17 boarding and 201 day schools; also a number of seminaries of learning of very creditable grades. The number of pupils attending the boarding-schools is 1,316, and the number attending the day schools is 6,546. The cost of maintaining these schools per annum is $196,612. Of this sum the Indians pay $175,071, and religious societies $21,541.

They have regularly organized governments, legislative, executive and judicial. Their officers are elective. They have churches of various denominations. I need not add they are self-supporting.

Now, a question arises, and to it I call the careful and thoughtful consideration of all who read this article. In 1856 I made treaties with four of those civilized tribes. Suppose I had been able to convince them, as I did their brethren west of Missouri, that it would promote their interests and advance their civilization to accept lands in severalty, the sale of the residue of their lands and the dissolution of the tribal relation, what would be their condition to-day? Could they have escaped the sad, sad fate which befell their brethren with whom I made treaties in 1854 and 1855?

When I made those treaties I was confident that good results would follow. Had I not so believed I would not have been a party to the transactions. Events following the execution of these treaties proved that I had committed a grave error. I had provided for the abrogation of the reservations, the dissolution of the tribal relation, and for lands in severalty and citizenship; thus making the road clear for the rapacity of the white man. I had broken down every barrier. I had committed a grevious mistake, and entailed on the Indians a legacy of cruel wrong and injury. Had I known then, as I now know, what would result from those treaties, I would be compelled to admit that I had committed a high crime.

Geo. W. Manypenny.

Washington, D.C., *Oct.* 20, 1885.

9

The General Allotment Act of 1887 ("The Dawes Act")

The text of the General Allotment Act, both in its inclusions and exclusions, reflected the ten-year debate discussed in the body of this work. It marked a turning point in Indian affairs: a compulsory turning away from tribal government and tribal autonomy, and from traditional cultural, economic and social values; a compulsory turning toward white social and economic values and laws to which the individual Indian was to be increasingly subjected. The act's omission of any provision authorizing leasing of the lands allotted was modified by acts of 1891, 1894, and 1897 which provided for such leases to white men under certain conditions (*Alternatives 4 and 5*).

Document†

—An Act to Provide for the Allotment of Lands in Severalty to Indians on the Various Reservations, and to Extend the Protection of the Laws of the United States and the Territories Over the Indians, and for Other Purposes

BE IT ENACTED *by the Senate and House of Representatives of the United States of America in Congress assembled*, That in all cases where any tribe or band of Indians has been, or shall hereafter be, located upon any reservation created for their use, either by treaty stipulation or by virtue of an act of Congress or executive order setting apart the same for their use, the President of the United States be, and he hereby is, authorized, whenever in his opinion any reservation or any part thereof of such Indians is advantageous for agricultural and grazing purposes, to cause said reservation, or any part thereof, to be surveyed, or resurveyed if necessary, and to allot the lands in said reservation in severalty to any Indian located thereon in

†From: U.S., *Statutes at Large*, vol. 24, pp. 388-91.

quantities as follows:
To each head of a family, one-quarter of a section;
To each single person over eighteen years of age, one-eighth of a section;
To each orphan child under eighteen years of age, one-eighth of a section; and
To each other single person under eighteen years now living, or who may be born prior to the date of the order of the President directing an allotment of the lands embraced in any reservation, one-sixteenth of a section: *Provided*, That in case there is not sufficient land in any of said reservations to allot lands to each individual of the classes above named in quantities as above provided, the lands embraced in such reservation or reservations shall be allotted to each individual of each of said classes pro rata in accordance with the provisions of this act: *And provided further*, That where the treaty or act of Congress setting apart such reservation provides for the allotment of lands in severalty in quantities in excess of those herein provided, the President, in making allotments upon such reservation, shall allot the lands to each individual Indian belonging thereon in quantity as specified in such treaty or act: *And provided further*, That when the lands allotted are only valuable for grazing purposes, an additional allotment of such grazing lands, in quantities as above provided, shall be made to each individual.

SECTION II

That all allotments set apart under the provisions of this act shall be selected by the Indians, heads of families selecting for their minor children, and the agents shall select for each orphan child, and in such manner as to embrace the improvements of the Indians making the selection. Where the improvements of two or more Indians have been made on the same legal subdivision of land, unless they shall otherwise agree, a provisional line may be run dividing said lands between them, and the amount to which each is entitled shall be equalized in the assignment of the remainder of the land to which they are entitled under this act. *Provided*, That if any one entitled to an allotment shall fail to make a selection within four years after the President shall direct that allotments may be made on a particular reservation, the Secretary of the Interior may direct the agent of such tribe or band, if such there be, and if there by no agent, than a special agent appointed for that purpose, to make a selection for such Indian, which election shall be allotted as in cases where selections are made by the Indians, and patents shall issue in like manner.

SECTION III

That the allotments provided for in this act shall be made by special agents appointed by the President for such purpose, and the agents in charge of the respective reservations on which the allotments are directed to be made, under such rules and regulations as the Secretary of the Interior may from time to time prescribe, and shall be certified by such agents to the Commissioner of Indian Affairs, in duplicate, one copy to be retained in the Indian Office and the other to be transmitted to the Secretary of the Interior for his action, and to be deposited in the General Land Office.

SECTION IV

That where any Indian not residing upon a reservation, or for whose tribe no reservation has been provided by treaty, act of Congress, or executive order, shall make settlement upon any surveyed or unsurveyed lands of the United States not otherwise appropriated, he or she shall be entitled, upon application to the local land-office for the district in which the lands are located, to have the same allotted to him or her, and to his or her children, in quantities and manner as provided in this act for Indians residing upon reservations; and when such settlement is made upon unsurveyed lands, the grant to such Indians shall be adjusted upon the survey of the lands so as to conform thereto; and patents shall be issued to them for such lands in the manner and with the restrictions as herein provided. And the fees to which the officers of such local land-office would have been entitled had such lands been entered under the general laws for the disposition of the public lands shall be paid to them, from any moneys in the Treasury of the United States not otherwise appropriated, upon a statement of an account in their behalf for such fees by the Commissioner of the General Land Office, and a certification of such account to the Secretary of the Treasury by the Secretary of the Interior.

SECTION V

That upon the approval of the allotments provided for in this act by the Secretary of the Interior, he shall cause patents to issue therefor in the name of the allottees, which patents shall be of the legal effect, and declare that the United States does and will hold the land thus allotted, for the period of twenty-five years, in trust for the sole use and benefit of the Indian to whom such allotment shall have been made, or, in case of his decease, of his heirs according to the laws of the State or Territory where such land is located, and that at the expiration of said period the United States will convey the same by patent to said Indian, or his heirs as aforesaid, in fee, discharged of said trust and free of all charge or incumbrance whatsoever: *Provided*, That the President of the United States may in any case in his discretion extend the period. And if any conveyance shall be made of the lands set apart and allotted as herein provided, or any contract made touching the same, before the expiration of the time above mentioned, such conveyance or contract shall be absolutely null and void:

Provided, That the law of descent and partition in force in the State or Territory where such lands are situate shall apply thereto after patents therefor have been executed and delivered, except as herein otherwise provided; and the laws of the State of Kansas regulating the descent and partition of real estate shall, so far as practicable, apply to all lands in the Indian Territory which may be allotted in severalty under the provisions of this act: *And provided further*, That at any time after lands have been allotted to all the Indians of any tribe as herein provided, or sooner if in the opinion of the President it shall be for the best interests of said tribe, it shall be lawful for the Secretary of the Interior to negotiate with such Indian tribe for the purchase and release by said tribe, in conformity with the treaty or statute under which such reservation is held, of such portions of its reservation not allotted as such tribe shall, from time to time, consent to sell, on such terms and conditions as shall be considered just and equitable between the United States and said tribe of Indians, which purchase shall not be complete until ratified by Congress, and the form and manner of executing such release shall also be prescribed by Congress: *Provided however*, That all lands adapted to agriculture, with or without irrigation so sold or released to the United States by any Indian tribe shall be held by the United States for the sole purpose of securing homes to actual settlers only in tracts not exceeding one hundred and sixty acres to any one person, on such terms as Congress shall prescribe, subject to grants which Congress may make in aid of education: *And provided further*, That no patents shall issue therefor except to the person so taking the same as and for a homestead, or his heirs, and after the expiration of five years occupancy thereof as such homestead; and any conveyance of said lands so taken as a homestead, or any contract touching the same, or lien thereon, created prior to the date of such patent, shall be null and void. And the sums agreed to be paid by the United States as purchase money for any portion of any such reservation shall be held in the Treasury of the United States for the sole use of the tribe or tribes of Indians; to whom such reservations belonged; and the same, with interest thereon at three percent per annum, shall be at all times subject to appropriation by Congress for the education and civilization of such tribe or tribes of Indians or the members thereof. The patents aforesaid shall be recorded in the General Land Office, and afterward delivered, free of charge, to the allottee entitled thereto. And if any religious society or other organization is now occupying any of the public lands to which this act is applicable, for religious or educational work among the Indians, the Secretary of the Interior is hereby authorized to confirm such occupation to such society or organization, in quantity not exceeding one hundred and sixty acres in any one tract, so long as the same shall be so occupied, on such terms as he shall deem just; but nothing herein contained shall change or alter any claim of such society for religious or educational purposes heretofore granted by law. And hereafter in the employment of Indian police, or any other employees in the public service among any of the Indian tribes or bands affected by this act, and where Indians can perform the duties required, those Indians who have availed themselves of the provisions of this act and become citizens of the United States shall be preferred.

SECTION VI

That upon the completion of said allotments and the presenting of the lands to said allottees, each and every member of the respective bands or tribes of Indians to whom allotments have been made shall have the benefit of and be subject to the laws, both civil and criminal, of the State or Territory in which they may reside; and no Territory shall pass or enforce any law denying any such Indian within its jurisdiction the equal protection of the law. And every Indian born within the territorial limits of the United States to whom allotments shall have been made under the provisions of this act, or under any law or treaty, and every Indian born within the territorial limits of the United States who has voluntarily taken up, within said limits, his residence separate and apart from any tribe of Indians therein, and has adopted the habits of civilized life, is hereby declared to be a citizen of the United States, and is entitled to all the rights, privileges, and immunities of such citizens, whether said Indian has been or not, by birth or otherwise, a member of any tribe of Indians within the territorial limits of the United States without in any manner impairing or otherwise affecting the right of any such Indian to tribal or other property.

SECTION VII

That in cases where the use of water for irrigation is necessary to render the lands within any Indian reservation available for agricultural purposes, the Secretary of the Interior be, and he is hereby, authorized to prescribe such rules and regulations as he may deem necessary to secure a just and equal distribution thereof among the Indians residing upon any such reservations; and no other appropriation or grant of water by any riparian proprietor shall be authorized or permitted to the damage of any other riparian proprietor.

SECTION VIII

That the provision of this act shall not extend to the territory occupied by the Cherokees, Creeks, Choctaws, Chickasaws, Seminoles, and Osage, Miamies and Peorias, and Sacs and Foxes, in the Indian Territory, nor to any of the reservations of the Seneca Nation of New York Indians in the State of New York, nor to that strip of territory in the State of Nebraska adjoining the Sioux Nation on the south added by executive order.

SECTION IX

That for the purpose of making the surveys and resurveys mentioned in section two of this act, there be, and hereby is, appropriated, out of any moneys in the Treasury not otherwise appropriated, the sum of one hundred thousand dollars, to be repaid proportionately out of the proceeds of the sales of such land as may be acquired from the Indians under the provisions of this act.

SECTION X

That nothing in this act contained shall be so construed as to affect the right and power of Congress to grant the right of way through any lands granted to an Indian, or a tribe of Indians, for railroads or other highways, or telegraph lines, for the public use, or to condemn such lands to public uses, upon making just compensation.

SECTION XI

That nothing in this act shall be so construed as to prevent the removal of the Southern Ute Indians from their present reservation in Southwestern Colorado to a new reservation by and with the consent of a majority of the adult male members of said tribe.

Approved, February 8, 1887.

Bibliographic Essay

The most thorough consideration of the events leading to the Dawes Act is Loring Benson Priest, *Uncle Sam's Stepchildren: The Reformation of United States Indian Policy, 1865-1887* (New Brunswick, N. J., 1942). Written as a doctoral dissertation at Harvard under Frederick Merk in the midst of the debate over the act's successor, the Indian Reorganization Act of 1934, Priest's book is marked by a detailed examination of the sources but reveals an uncritical commitment to the cause of Indian assimilation and a cultural insensitivity to Indian values.

An earlier work, Jay P. Kinney, *A Continent Lost—A Civilization Won: Indian Land Tenure in America* (Baltimore, 1937), is based on a detailed consideration of the primary documents. Kinney emphasizes the purity of the motives of the humanitarians responsible for the Dawes Act and minimizes the role of railroads, landgrabbers, and others with more selfish motives.

Henry E. Fritz, *The Movement for Indian Assimilation, 1860-1890* (Philadelphia, 1963), deals mostly with the "Peace Policy" of General Grant, and his consideration of the origins of the Dawes Act is brief. However, Fritz provides a useful corrective to some of the views of Priest and Kinney. Fritz is currently working on a history of the late nineteenth-century reformers.

The most recent study of the humanitarian reform movement leading to the Dawes Act is Robert Winston Mardock, *The Reformers and the American Indian* (Columbia, Mo., 1971). Mardock's work covers the entire period from the Civil War to the Dawes Act and differs in emphasis from both Priest's and Fritz's books.

Francis Paul Prucha, who is presently working on a history of United States Indian policy in the last half of the nineteenth century, has edited a useful documentary collection entitled *Americanizing the American Indian: Writings by the "Friends of the Indian" 1880-1900* (Cambridge, Mass., 1973), which deals with some of the published views of governmental and nongovernmental leaders on the subject of a general allotment law.

Prucha has also edited Delos Sacket Otis's study of the Dawes Act, originally published in 1934 in a little-used government document, in an updated edition under the title *The Dawes Act and the Allotment of Indian Lands* (Norman, Okla., 1973).

General histories of the American Indian deal fleetingly with the Dawes Act. Angie Debo's *A History of the Indians of the United States* (Norman, Okla., 1970), discusses the general allotment legislation in Chapter 16, "Breaking Up the Reservation," pp. 251-267, but deals principally with the allotment problem in Oklahoma in the 1890s and 1900s.

The role of the railroads in the agitation for the breakup of reservations and the allotment of land in severalty is an uncertain one. Some data, particularly in the early period of railroad building, is incorporated in Paul Wallace Gates, *Fifty Million Acres: Conflicts Over Kansas Land Policy, 1854-1890* (Ithaca, N. Y., 1954), and in Ira G. Clark, *Then Came the Railroads: The Century from Steam to Diesel in the Southwest* (Norman, Okla., 1958).

Important articles on land allotment include Theodore H. Haas "The Legal Aspects of Indian Affairs from 1887 to 1957," a special issue on American Indians and American Life, edited by George F. Simpson and J. Milton Yinger, in *The Annals of the American Academy of Political and Social Science*, 311 (May 1957): 12-22; and Allan G. Harper, "Salvaging the Wreckage of Indian Land Allotment," in *The Changing Indian*, edited by Oliver LaFarge, (Norman, Okla., 1943), pp. 84-102.

Basic source documents dealing with the origins of the Dawes Act include the *Annual Reports of the Board of Indian Commissioners*, the *Annual Reports of the Commissioner of Indian Affairs*, the variously titled annual reports of the *Lake Mohonk Conferences*, held at Lake Mohonk, New York, *in behalf of the Civilization and Legal Protection of the Indians of the United States* (Philadelphia, 1883 and subsequent years), the pamphlets and reports issued by the Indian Rights Association of Philadelphia (1882 to the present), and *The Council Fire*, a monthly journal begun in Philadelphia in January 1878 under the editorial management of A. B. Meacham, and later edited by T. A. Bland in Washington, D.C. Another important source is the *Speeches, Correspondence and Political Papers of Carl Schurz*, edited by Frederic Bancroft, 6 vols. (New York, 1913, reprinted 1969). *The American Indian and the United States: A Documentary History*, edited by Wilcomb E. Washburn, 4 vols. (New York, 1973), provides excerpts from congressional debates, reports of commissioners of Indian affairs, and other documents bearing on the allotment question.

Important manuscript sources for a study of the movement culminating in the General Allotment Act are the Henry L. Dawes and Carl Schurz papers in the Manuscript Division of the Library of Harvard University, the Henry M. Teller papers in the Denver, Colorado, Public Library, and the Alice Fletcher papers in the National Anthropological Archives of the Smithsonian Institution.

A seventy-four page typescript account of "The Origins of the Dawes Act of 1887" by Samuel Taylor, Philip Washburn Prize Thesis, Harvard University, 1927, in the Harvard University Archives, documents the western interest in the passage of the Dawes Act more fully than does the published literature.

Larry E. Burgess, "The Lake Mohonk Conferences on the Indian, 1883-1916," Ph.D. dissertation, Claremont Graduate School, 1972, recounts the proceedings of the conferences in a rather perfunctory way, relying for the most part on the published records of the conference. An abridgement of Burgess's work is in preparation by the Clearwater Publishing Company, Inc., 50 Rockefeller Plaza, New York, N.Y. 10020, in an index volume accompanying a microfiche edition of the annual reports of the conference.

Marshall Dwight Moody, "A History of the Board of Indian Commissioners and its Relationship to the Administration of Indian Affairs, 1869-1900," Master's thesis, American University, 1951, is a brief (115 typewritten pages) summary of the work of the Board, organized by subjects such as land, civilization and education, reservation problems and the like, based largely on the published reports of the board.

Everett Arthur Gilcreast, "Richard Henry Pratt and American Indian Policy, 1877-1906: A Study of the Assimilation Movement," Ph.D. dissertation, Yale University, 1967, is a thorough and detailed study showing sympathy to Pratt and hostility to the humanitarian reformers.

Henry George Waltmann, "The Interior Department, War Department and Indian Policy, 1865-1887," Ph.D. dissertation, University of Nebraska, 1962, concentrates on the continuing debate between advocates of War Department control of the Indians and Interior Department control, but contains a useful chapter on the Dawes Act.

Fred H. Nicklason, "The Early Career of Henry L. Dawes, 1816-1871," Ph.D. dissertation, Yale University, 1967, does not deal with the career of Dawes during the severalty battle, but provides important background information on his career as an Indian reformer.

Edward Sterl Phinney, "Alfred B. Meacham, Promoter of Indian Reform," Ph.D. dissertation, University of Oregon, 1963, asserts that Meacham, founder of the *Council Fire*, had a greater influence on Indian reform than is usually accorded him, and rejects some of the aspersions cast on him by Loring B. Priest.

George W. Manypenny's *Our Indian Wards*, first published in Cincinnati in 1880, and Helen Hunt Jackson's *A Century of Dishonor* (New York, 1881), were both important factors in producing the conviction that the Indian system needed reform. Manypenny's book has been reissued (New York, 1972) with a new foreword by Henry E. Fritz. Jackson's book has been reprinted (New York, 1965), with an introduction by Andrew F. Rolle.

The role of Richard Henry Pratt in the formulation of Indian policy in the late nineteenth century is skillfully told in *Battlefield and Classroom: Four Decades with the American Indian, 1867-1904* by Richard Henry Pratt, edited by Robert M. Utley (New Haven, 1964).

Alice Fletcher, the pioneer anthropologist who involved herself in the fight for Omaha severalty legislation, is discussed by Nancy Oestreich Lurie in a chapter entitled "Women in Early American Anthropology," in *Pioneers of American Anthropology: The Uses of Biography* edited by June Helm (Seattle, 1966), pp. 29-81. Alice Fletcher's own scholarly output includes the monumental 654-page "The Omaha Tribe," with Francis LaFlesche, prepared for the Smithsonian Institution, Bureau of American Ethnology, *Annual Report* 27 (1905-1906) (actually published in 1911) and the equally voluminous 693-page report prepared for the U. S. Office of Education, in response to Senate Resolution of February 23, 1885, entitled *Indian Education and Civilization*, 48th Cong., 2d sess., Ex. Doc. No. 95 (Washington, 1888).

The special quality of the Lake Mohonk "House"—where liquor, dancing, card playing, and Sabbath breaking were silently prohibited by the Quaker Smiley brothers, has been lovingly recounted by Frederick E. Partington, *The Story of Mohonk* (Fulton, N. Y., 1911; 2d ed. 1932), and also by Lyman Abbott in a sketch of "The Smiley Brothers: Lovers of Hospitality," in *Silhouettes of My Contemporaries* (Garden City, N. Y., 1921), pp. 28-44, and in an appreciation of Albert K. Smiley on his death in *The Outlook* 102 no. 15 (December 14, 1912): 801-3. Abbott's own work with the Indians is evaluated by himself in his *Reminiscences* (Boston, 1915, reprinted 1923), pp. 425-29; and by Ira V. Brown, *Lyman Abbott, Christian Evolutionist: A Study in Religious Liberalism* (Cambridge, Mass., 1953), pp. 89-98.

6 -300

DATE DUE

KF5660
.W38

Washburn

The assault on Indian tribalism